ANCIENT CHINA

An Illustrated Introduction to the History, People, Culture and Beyond

ANCIENT CHINA

An Illustrated Introduction to the
History, People, Culture *and* **Beyond**

By Zou Yi, Zhang Zhaoyang and Li Biyan
Translated by Jiang Yajun

SCPG

Text and Images: Zou Yi, Zhang Zhaoyang, and Li Biyan
Translation: Jiang Yajun

Cover Design: Wang Wei
Interior Design: Li Jing and Hu Bin (Yuan Yinchang Design Studio)

Copy Editor: Nick Choa
Assistant Editors: Cao Yue, Yang Wenjing
Editor: Wu Yuezhou

ISBN: 978-1-63288-026-0

Address any comments about *Ancient China* to:

SCPG
401 Broadway, Ste. 1000
New York, NY 10013
USA

or

Shanghai Press and Publishing Development Co., Ltd.
Floor 5, No. 390 Fuzhou Road, Shanghai, China (200001)
Email: sppd@sppdbook.com

Printed in China by Shanghai Donnelley Printing Co., Ltd.

1   3   5   7   9   10   8   6   4   2

CFP offers the images on pages 29, 33, 38, 40, 43–45, 56, 57, 60, 70–73, 79, 81, 82, 84, 90–92, 100, 106, 123, 126, 127, 132, 135, 138, 140, 142, 143, 148–151, 156, and 159.

On pages 1–3

Figs. 1–2 *A Thousand Miles of Rivers and Mountains*

Wang Ximeng (b. 1096)
Ink and color on silk
Length 1191.5 cm, height 51.5 cm
The Palace Museum, Beijing

Regarded as one of the best among traditional Chinese landscape paintings, this piece evokes a sense of peace and prosperity. It reflects the ideal world with perfect order and harmony according to the emperor's will.

CONTENTS

CONTENTS

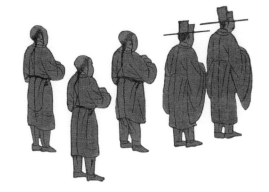

On the facing page

Fig. 3 The complete scroll of *Tribute of the Myriad Nations*. Please refer to fig. 111 on page 155 for the painting information.

Introduction

Like other early civilizations on Earth, the ancient Chinese civilization was born on a land with rivers meandering through fertile open fields—an ideal geographical setting considered the cradle of early agricultural communities and civilizations.

The Yangtze River and the Yellow River, China's main waterways, rank among the longest in the world. Equally renowned within the country are the two mighty rivers' numerous tributaries, such as the Wei River and Fen River in the north and the Huai River and Han River in the south. These "great rivers" have evoked awe and respect among the Chinese people from a very early period. For a long time in history, both at official and civil levels, elaborate sacrificial rituals were performed to honor and worship these waterways.

Great mountains are also objects of worship. The "Five Sacred Mountains," named

On pages 8–11

Figs. 4–5 Details of *Along the River During the Qingming Festival*. Please refer to fig. 63 on page 107 for more information of the painting.

after the five cardinal directions (with the center among them), stand among the most revered natural landmarks in the country. In comparison to these five mountains in the Han culture, the Tianshan, Qilian, Kunlun, Himalaya, and Hengduan mountains in the west, as well as the Altai, Yin, and Greater Khingan mountains in the north, hold even greater geographical significance for China. They not only contribute to China's staircase-like terrain, descending gradually from west to east, but also act as a natural demarcation line between early civilizations of agriculture and nomadism.

While great rivers and mountains form varying geographical units and environments, mountain and river valleys were often better places for early people to settle down and, more importantly, made it easier for them to communicate with one another.

This constitutes the fundamental geographical landscape of China, which has borne witness to its rich and captivating history in ancient times.

Fig. 6   T-Shaped Painting on Silk from Tomb No. I at Mawangdui (detail)
Width 92 cm
Hunan Provincial Museum

This piece served as a funeral banner and was found in the Mawangdui Tombs in Changsha, Hunan Province, China. The painting displays the way the ancient people perceived the concepts of Heaven, the human world, and the Netherworld. The upper section here features a red sun and a crescent moon, with a crow in the sun and a tree under it. Among the branches of the tree are eight smaller suns. Between the sun and the moon in the top corners, there is a woman with a human head and a snake's body, who is Nüwa (see detail on the facing page). This celestial scene represents the depiction of Nüwa by later generations.

CHAPTER ONE
Age of Gods:
Prehistory

When did the first population of modern humans, known as Homo sapiens, colonize the land where China is today? Did they originate in Africa? Answering such questions relies on research into fossils from ancient human ancestors in and outside China and their traditions and cultures of chipping and using stone tools. Remains of Homo erectus, primates intermediate between man and the anthropoid apes, and early humans were unearthed in different places in China. While the dating of certain sites and, particularly, the nature of the fossils and stone tools believed to be from 1,000,000 BP, are still open to debate, ancient hominid sites which chip and use stone tools dated between 1,500,000 BP and 50,000 BP in South China and in central and eastern China, particularly in the middle and lower Yangtze River and Yellow River basins, show distinct cultural patterns in terms of stoneware features.

How do we define "China" and its people, "the Chinese," in the context of new cultural sites that have emerged since 50,000 BP, when stone-made artifacts were no longer dominant? Before answering this question, let's turn to Chinese mythology that speaks to the origin of humanity.

Mother of Humans

In Chinese mythology, before the universe was created, there was absolutely nothing but chaotic darkness. It was Pangu, a cosmic being that first emerged in it, who separated the sky and the earth, but in between no humans existed. Nüwa, a Chinese deity, took clumps of yellow earth and molded them into human figures. Unfortunately, the work left her too exhausted to finish her creation with her bare hands, so she dragged a cord through the mud and lifted it out. The drops that fell on the ground became individual human beings.

Nüwa's myth is one of the oldest stories in Chinese mythology, dating back at least to the Warring States period (475–221 BC). With a deity as the central figure and earth as the material, the myth is regarded by some historians as a metaphor for the distinctive traits of early Chinese civilization (fig. 6).

About 13,000 years ago, the global geography, climate, and species began undergoing drastic changes towards what they are today. With the Ice Age coming to an end, the global climate was warming, and sea levels were rising and, as a result, large animals like mammoths went extinct. Human hunters had to turn to smaller animals. While men were responsible for hunting and fishing, women took on the tasks of gathering edible leaves, fruits, and insects. Despite the different responsibilities shouldered by each gender, both tasks were equally important for them to feed themselves, although hunting is assumed to be mostly secondary. Stones, abundant everywhere, served as the primary source for manufacturing production tools. The land, beyond being used for habitation, had few other purposes, and most of the time there was no surplus of a day's harvest. Collective labor remained predominant. Whether in households or tribes, members were relatively equal, with women enjoying the same freedom and rights as men. However, women were revered and honored for their ability to bear children. For early societies, the ability to reproduce was far more important than productivity. The more children a woman had, the more respect she received in the tribe, elevating her status. This is the matriarchal structure of early communities that Nüwa myth reflects, depicting the status of women in society and the significance of their reproductive capabilities. Nüwa, therefore, is portrayed in the myth as the ancient "grandmother" of the Chinese nation.

Also symbolic in Nüwa's myth is earth, which can be interpreted as a reflection of the invention of pottery-making technology in prehistorical culture in China.

Excavations in North, Central, and South China yielded pottery that dated back over 10,000 years. In fact, pottery appeared relatively early throughout East Asia, not only in China. As large mammals died out with the warming climate at the end of the Ice Age, the reduced hunting options compelled humans to migrate to lowland forest areas with more nut-bearing trees. The new

lifestyle of gathering nuts, fish and shells led to the invention of pottery, which not only allowed for secure storage of food but was used in cooking.

The pivotal role pottery played in China's prehistoric culture lies not only in its early presence but also in its association with the advent of agriculture and the presence of permanent settlements. In contrast, in regions such as West Asia, agriculture started much earlier than pottery making, while in others, including Japan, pottery vessels were used in settled communities long before agricultural life.

Archaeological evidence from China suggests that agriculture started first in the middle and lower Yangtze River basins, which are the birthplaces of rice agriculture. In fact, this region was already on the periphery where the wild rice grew. The low yield in gathering of the progenitor led to the earliest attempts to farm rice to meet demand. In sites in Hunan and Jiangxi provinces in the middle Yangtze River basin, the earliest pottery fragments in China dating back to 13,000 BP were unearthed, along with the discovery of cultivated rice, which was bred using wild rice.

Even today, rice remains the staple crop in South China, a tradition that has persisted for over 10,000 years. In contrast, the northerners primarily consume wheat, which is mainly made into mantou (steamed buns), jiaozi (Chinese dumplings), and noodles. However, research shows that the earliest crop during the Neolithic era in the northern regions, typically in the middle and lower Yellow River basin, was millet. The grain is drought-resistant, has strong self-sustainability, and grows well in the loose and fertile loess soil typical of the area. Little is known about how it was domesticated in the first place, but sites containing grains of millet and concerning millet-related activities dating back to approximately 6,000 to 7,000 BP have been discovered from time to time in Hebei,

Henan, and Gansu provinces respectively in North China, East China, and northwestern China. Millstones and grinding rods used for processing grains have also been found.

With agriculture becoming the primary source of food, the range of activities naturally narrowed down, and humans experienced a switch from a nomadic to a settled way of life. The settled life, in turn, provided an unprecedented favorable condition for women to give birth to and raise children. Pottery, made from readily available clay, was not only highly favored by ancient Chinese people for its practicality but also provided a means for them to document their artistic creativity (fig. 7).

This is a thumbnail sketch of the historical background of early Chinese

Fig. 7   Painted Pottery Jar with Stork, Fish, and Stone Axe Designs

Yangshao Culture, Neolithic Age
Height 47 cm
National Museum of China, Beijing

This pottery jar is an urn burial vessel from the Yangshao culture, used to store or offer the belongings of the deceased. The surface of the pottery jar is painted with intricate designs, reflecting the artistic expression and thoughtful composition of subjects by people in ancient times.

civilization, representing the basic situation of a matriarchal community in China, as the matriarchal community thrived about 7,000 to 8,000 years ago until it switched to a patriarchy about 2,000 years later. Archaeological sites reflecting matriarchies are scattered across China, numbering in the thousands, with dozens of them having been designated as archaeological cultures. Most of these sites covered a rather long span in history, and some represented a transition from a matriarchal society to a patriarchal one or, even, to a civilized one. In comparison to stone tools, agricultural evidence, pottery, tombs, settlements, and burial items in this period have received even more attention from archaeologists.

Besides creating humans, Nüwa is also known in China for her sincere care for them. In another myth about Nüwa, human beings led a peaceful life for a long time until one day the pillar of the sky fell down, turning the world into chaos. The sky began to crack and torrential water falling through the developing holes turned into fierce floods sweeping across all lands. The ground split, the scalding magma splattered. Meanwhile, great fires broke out and raged in all directions. To make things worse, savage beasts and vicious birds came out to prey on helpless human beings. Seeing the dreadful disaster her offspring experienced, Nüwa was determined to save humanity. She collected stones of five colors, melted them in the fire, and climbed up the mountain to mend the holes in the sky. Being afraid of the sky's collapse again, she cut off the four legs of a giant turtle she found underwater and took them as pillars to support the sky. She calmed the floods and killed the savage beasts and vicious birds. Finally, the world restored its peace and tranquilness.

This legend, from another perspective, showcases the courage and wisdom of female tribal leaders in a matriarchal society, the prelude to Chinese civilization.

Age of Heroes

The matrilineal nature of the hierarchical social structure is reflected in ancient documents stating that children at that time "knew who their mothers were but not their fathers," reflecting the practice of children taking their mother's surname. As humans switched from hunting and gathering to farming, the competitive advantage of men, who were in general physically tougher than women, became increasingly apparent. In addition to the contribution of manual labor in agricultural production, with the increasing conflicts and unavoidable wars between tribes, the division of labor by gender became more pronounced.

As a result, in titling the head of a group, the character "王 (king)," the pictograph resembling an ax in oracle bone script, was chosen (fig. 8). It was through the ax, a farming tool as well as a weapon, that males gained more power in politics and decision-making. Eventually, matriarchy collapsed into patriarchy, leaving men and their male gods ruling society's values and structures. As an era of constant conflict and integration among tribes, the patriarchal society in China left behind numerous heroic deeds and figures, gradually ushering in the beginning of Chinese civilization.

Among them is Huangdi (Emperor Huang), commonly known as the Yellow Emperor, who is reputed to have been born about 2704 BC and to have begun his rule as emperor in 2697 BC. Ancestor of several tribes in the middle Yellow River basin, he is credited with defeating another large tribe in Wei River basin, ruled by Yan Emperor, and formed an alliance with them, which became the most powerful military group in northern China. The Yan-Huang alliance is of great significance to the Chinese people, subsequent rulers in the whole of the Yellow River basin acknowledged Yan-Huang as their common ancestor. They believed that

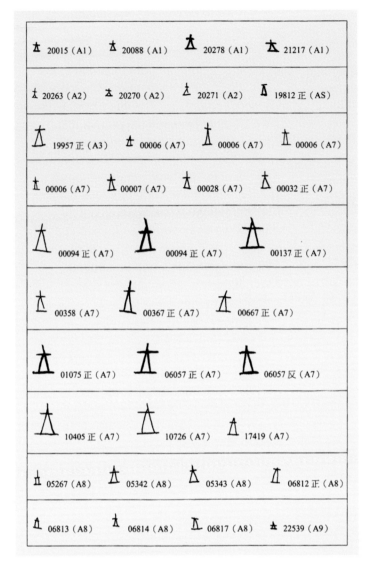

Fig. 8 The different Chinese characters of "王(king)" presented in oracle bone inscriptions.

their common sense of kinship. Today, the Chinese, especially the Han people, commonly refer to themselves as the "descendants of Yan-Huang" or the "People of Huaxia Origin." When the Qingming Festival, also known as Tomb Sweeping Day, is celebrated in early April by Chinese people to remember and honor ancestors, public commemorative events are held at the mausoleums of Yellow Emperor and Yan Emperor, in China's northwestern Shaanxi and south-central Hunan provinces, respectively.

Unity in Diversity

The vast land occupied by China is characterized by dramatic geographical diversity. Archaeological remains left by early people in various periods, from the early stages of human evolution a million years ago to the heroic era, have been unearthed across the country. It is believed that, while regional archaeological cultures developed in their own fashions, they influenced others and were influenced. While historians and folklorists primarily rely on resources in historical records and mythological literature to trace the origins of early humans, archaeologists use tools like shovels, trowels, spades, and brushes to search for traces that human ancestors left and attempt to establish correspondences between archaeological evidence and written records.

the legendary sages such as Yao, Shun, and Yu, even if they are not the direct descendants or have a blood relationship with the Yellow Emperor, are all related to the Yan-Huang alliance.

The generations of rulers since the Yellow Emperor armed their subjects in central China with a sense of shared identity and defeated the Dongyi tribe in eastern China and the Sanmiao tribe in the middle Yangtze River basin, becoming the most powerful tribal alliance in China at that time. At the same time, the victories helped heighten

The rule of the Yan-Huang tribal alliance continued in the vast period until the birth of ancient Chinese civilization. The earliest Chinese dynasties—Xia (2070–1600 BC),

Shang (1600–1046 BC), and Zhou (1046–256 BC)—are believed to be established by Yan-Huang decedents. This, of course, doesn't mean that the founders were the direct descendants of the Yan and Yellow emperors. Nor does it mean that the Yan-Huang tribes have no other descendants besides Xia, Shang and Zhou. It cannot even be said that in ancient China, apart from the Yan-Huang tribes, there were no other powerful tribes and their descendants. So, how can we prove the historicity of other tribes and their relationship with the Xia, Shang, and Zhou dynasties?

Ever since the 1980s, archaeological evidence has been accumulating, pointing to the historicity of pre-historical cultures in the Yangtze River basin. These cultures might have been as impressive as those in the Yellow River basin. How and why did they vanish before the existence of written records? The historical records of the defeat of the Sanmiao tribe by the Yan-Huang alliance has led archaeologists and historians to speculate that the tribes in the middle Yangtze River basin may have suffered devastating blows from the external cultures including tribes of the middle Yellow River basin, creating huge gaps in archeological cultural continuity. In addition, artifacts from a different culture or elements with traits from a different culture have often been found in some cultural sites. For example, some artifact styles in archaeological remains of the Huaxia tribe in the middle Yellow River basin and the Dongyi tribe in the lower Yellow River basin show strong influence from each other. These may well be the products of warfare or other forms of exchange.

This reminds us of the fact that many ancient legendary stories and histories were written by conquerors. The theory that Chinese culture originated from a single source was proposed and reinforced by the early Huaxia tribe living in the middle Yellow River basin and Wei River region in order to strengthen their political power and shape their ethnic identity. Instead, based on archaeological discoveries, the origin of Chinese civilization is likely diverse. Even after entering the civilized period, many smaller tribes and kingdoms coexisted around the Xia, Shang, and Zhou dynasties. The relationships between these groups and the more powerful Chinese dynasties were complicated, involving alliances, subordination, or shifting allegiances based on each other's changing strengths. The concept of the Chinese empire as we understand it today did not exist. The traditional notion that "the Xia, Shang, Zhou were the dynasties ruling China" is a much later construct; their rule was limited to specific cultural regions. This is why some archaeologists have proposed the theory of "unity in diversity," suggesting that the origin and formation of ancient Chinese civilization should be approached as a continuous process. How China integrated from various cultural regions into a centralized state will be discussed later.

Megaflood Myth

Common in many world mythologies are stories about world-ending floods, and the Chinese one is no exception. According to *Shiji* (also known as *Records of the Grand Historian*) by Sima Qian (c. 145 BC–?), a Chinese historian of the Han dynasty (202 BC–AD 220) and the father of Chinese histography, a great flood engulfed China during the reign of the legendary ruler of Huaxia tribal alliance named Emperor Yao, a great-great-grandson of the Yellow Emperor. Uprooted from their homes, the people fled uphill to escape the torrential waters, seeking shelter in mountain caves. Yao appointed, rather reluctantly, Gun, the head of a large tribe named Xia on the southern bank of the river, to tackle the floods. Both Gun and Gonggong, who led another major tribe on the northern bank, were experienced flood controllers, but they both were unsuccessful in winning the leadership of the Huaxia tribe. Gun spent nine years to have dams and embankments constructed in an attempt to combat the advancing floodwaters, but, unfortunately, his efforts proved futile.

After Yao, the leader of Huaxia was Shun. One of the reasons why Yao and Shun are revered as sage figures in Chinese culture is that both, during their lifetimes, passed on the position of tribal alliance leader to someone not directly related to them by blood. Legend has it that Shun was a distant relative of Yao but, more importantly, a wise and virtuous person, which won him the leadership. Evidently, Shun must have gained the support of all alliance members for the role.

As punishment, Gun was executed by Shun, and his son Yu, better known as Yu the Great, was ordered to step up to the plate in the wake of his father's failure. It seems a strange story, but it was the privileged status of Xia in the tribal alliance, led by Yao-Shun, and the role it played in the water control project that secured Yu the appointment, while his father was executed.

Instead of trying to contain the flood, Yu chose to divert it. He ordered channels to be dredged so the floodwaters would be drained away. The water problem was solved and, at the same time, more grains were produced. Yu was diligent and highly respected. Legend has it that he was so dedicated to his task of fighting the flood that he passed by his own family's doorstep three times, but each time he did not return inside to meet his wife, to whom he had been married only four days before saying goodbye. He convened a grand assembly of tribal leaders at Tushan Mountain, securing his position in the alliance of tribes. This event is considered a crucial milestone in the formal establishment of the Xia dynasty. Due to his achievements in flood control, Shun abdicated the position of alliance leader to him, creating another

inspiring story.

Archaeological evidence now points to new insight into the dramatic 4,000-year-old Chinese myth. The flood may have led a diversion of the Yellow River, greatly altering the physical environment in the core region of Huaxia. Some cultural sites from the same period might have been destroyed and, as a result, many archaeological cultures during this period exhibit discontinuities, and subsequent cultures show significant regression. Many cultural sites were basically abandoned during the same period. The project to tame the flood started where the tribe of Gonggong was located, an area most severely affected by the northern flow of the Yellow River. As the Yellow River changed its course, it became essential for people in the downstream region of the Yellow River and Huai River basins to prevent flood disasters. The reason why Gun was executed at Yushan (the present-day border of Shandong and Jiangsu provinces in East China) was because his flood control had actually utilized the soil resources in the Huai River basin, and it is reasonable to conclude that the Xia had conquered much of this southeastern region, but not the Tushan tribe. This explains why Yu the Great married the daughter of the head of the Tushan tribe and convened a grand assembly of tribal leaders at Tushan, to seek support for his flood control project and secure dominance over the region.

Several excavated ancient city sites in the central area of Xia tribe activity in the present west of Henan Province were likely important cities in the early years of the Xia dynasty. The gullies (i.e., grooves formed by intermittent water erosion on the earth's surface) discovered in some sites point to the relationship between the establishment of the Xia dynasty and Yu's flood management effort (see fig. 9 on the next page).

The significance of flood control in the formation of the early Chinese state lies in the crucial role it played in early agricultural societies. The water control effort by Yu is documented in *Shangshu* (also known as *Book of Documents*), a collection of rhetorical prose attributed to figures of ancient China. Documents from the Warring States period discovered in the past years have also revealed a link between Yu's project and the term "Jiuzhou" ("Nine States"), an early name for "China." The term is also a symbol of cultural regional unity, referring to the core area of Huaxia, where nine culturally different regions were united through the flood control effort. Yu's success, therefore, can be attributed to his method of basin-wide flood control, in contrast to his father's regional flood control. The massive water control covering the nine states could be a systematic engineering project requiring a significant amount of manpower, resources, strong leadership, and meticulous organizational management. The fact that a tribal head named Fangfeng was killed for being late for the grand assembly, convened by Yu, at Tushan, indicates what harsh discipline was exercised. At the same time, it shows what powerful authority Yu had established over other tribes in the whole of Jiuzhou, which led to the coming imperial dynasty of China.

After the death of Yu, his son Qi conquered the Dongyi tribe and killed its head, Yi. As Dongyi contributed significantly in Yu's water control project, it was likely that Yu would have hoped to pass the rulership to Yi, following the tradition of Yao and Shun. However, having gained much power in its leadership in the combined effort to survive the catastrophic flood disaster, Yu's tribe, Xia, was already aggressive enough to allow him made the hereditary ruler in his family, disregarding the practice of "abdication" (or passing on the position of tribal alliance leader to someone not directly related to them by blood) and opposing voices from other tribes. With the establishment of the first imperial dynasty, China entered a new era in terms of state form.

Fig. 9 Map of the Tracks of Yu the Great

Engraved during the Song dynasty (960–1279), this is one of the earliest existing stone-carved maps in China. It marks administrative regions, rivers, mountains, and lakes, depicting the transportation of tribute within the legendary domain of Yu the Great of the Xia dynasty (2070–1600 BC) and reflecting the significant role of Yu in the early stages of Chinese civilization.

CHAPTER TWO
A Change of Focus:
Shang and Zhou Dynasties

The Xia dynasty, founded by Yu the Great and Emperor Qi, is said to have been the first hereditary kingdom recorded in Chinese historical texts, marking the birth of Chinese civilization. Unfortunately, due to its ancient history, there is a considerable scarcity of historical records regarding the legendary first imperial dynasty. Based on the areas of activity recorded in early literature about Xia people, archaeologists have been working on the whereabouts of the earliest Chinese dynasty for several decades and, as a result, cultural remnants have been discovered in the western Henan Province and the southern Shanxi Province in North China. The periodic demarcation of these findings falls

On the facing page

Fig. 10　Mao Gong Ding

Late Western Zhou dynasty (1046–771 BC)
Height 53.8 cm, diameter 47 cm, weight 34.7 kg
Palace Museum, Taibei

This bronze ding (cauldron) has a robust shape with simple and unadorned decorations. It is renowned for its inscription, which is nearly 500 characters long, making it the longest inscription found on a bronze vessel. The inscription, which can be divided into seven sections, records that at the beginning of King Xuan of Zhou's reign, he was anxious to see the country thrive, and appointed his uncle, Duke Mao, to manage both internal and external affairs of the state, urging him to be diligent and selfless. Finally, he bestowed upon him official garments and generous gifts, and in response, Duke Mao cast the ding to pass down as an eternal treasure for his descendants. This complete narrative is an important historical source for studying the politics of the late Western Zhou period.

within or around the chronological range of the Xia dynasty. Although there is no firm evidence to substantiate such a linkage, the site is no doubt archaeologically impressive in terms of both scale and historicity.

While similar sites of the culture have been found in a large area across several provinces, a typical one is in Erlitou Site in the Luoyang Basin of Henan Province. Luoyang is known as "the ancient capital of nine dynasties" in Chinese history. The "nine" here does not refer to an exact number nine. In Chinese it is sometimes used to broadly indicate a large quantity, similar to the concept of the Jiuzhou mentioned in the previous chapter. Luoyang was chosen as capital in ancient China because of its location in what ancient Chinese people referred to as the "center of the world," the middle and lower Yangtze River basins where the Huaxia tribe lived. Why is the Luoyang Basin a crucial area for China's transition from the prehistoric era to the civilized era, or the earliest center in Chinese civilization history? The Erlitou Site provides the answer.

Erlitou is a site of a large state-level society in China; many artifacts and remnants have been discovered, which are believed to be the earliest ones in the history of East Asia. These findings are related to subsequent Chinese dynasties. Among the remains are China's earliest urban road network, earliest courtyard palace along a central axis, earliest imperial palace, earliest government-run handicraft workshop areas (including copper casting workshops and turquoise ware workshops), and the earliest rutting (traces of two-wheeled carts) in East Asia. It was also the first time that royal tombs have been discovered within a palace area, where the earliest primitive ceramics in China were found among the burial goods. In addition, the site yielded the earliest bronze battle-axe in China. Erlitou boasts many such "firsts" in China, indicating the emergence of a more powerful political entity in the Central Plains region than those in other regions. The reason why China is called the "Central Kingdom" can be traced back to the archaeological background of the Erlitou culture.

As exploration of the Xia culture continues to deepen, we will focus on the two dynasties that followed Xia—the Shang and the Zhou.

Early Shang and Zhou People

At the end of the Qing dynasty (1644–1911), oracle bone scripts were unearthed by local farmers in Anyang, China's Henan Province. In 1928, the source of the oracle bones was traced back to modern Xiaotun village in Anyang and an official archaeological excavation was carried out. The discoveries stunned the world. This site, dating back 3,300 years, was the political, economic, and cultural center of the late Shang dynasty for over 250 years: Yin.

Fig. II Oracle Bone with Chinese Characters

Shang dynasty (1600–1046 BC)
Yinxu Museum, Anyang, Henan Province

This is a fragment of an oracle bone, on which 93 individual characters were identified. The characters are clear, uniform in size, and incisively carved. The inscription on it records the Shang king's divination on a specific day regarding whether there would be calamities during hunting.

Yinxu (Ruins of Yin) have a grand scale, with surviving sites including palaces, temples, royal tombs, settlements, family graveyards, sacrificial pits, oracle bone pits, and workshops. Excavations have unearthed tens of thousands of exquisite artifacts, including oracle bones, bronze objects, jade artifacts, pottery, and bone implements. Most importantly, the discovery of oracle bone scripts conclusively confirms the existence of the Shang dynasty. It is because of the abundance of oracle bone scripts that the development of Chinese characters can be traced back to the Yin era. While the Chinese script may not be the oldest writing system in history, it is the only one that has been in continuous use for at least three to four millennia (fig. 11).

So, what was the Shang dynasty like before the era of the Yin period? Legend has it that the Shang people were a branch of the Huaxia ethnic group. In the early stages, they inhabited the vicinity of Shangqiu in eastern Henan Province. Unlike the mountainous and hilly western parts of Henan, this area, characterized by plains and marshes, is located downstream of the Yellow River. In the early period, the Shang people seemed to lead a "nomadic" life. However, unlike the typical nomadic lifestyle involving long-distance traveling and unsettled life, they moved only from the lower reaches of the Yellow River or even further southeast to the north bank of the river, specifically the northwestern Henan Province to the southern Hebei Province. The animals they herded were likely not the horses or sheep commonly associated with nomadic tribes, but rather water buffalo and the like.

During their migrations, the Shang people built settlements for agricultural production. However, compared to the agriculturally focused Zhou people, they were more likely to excel in trade. Some believe that the Chinese word for businessman, "shangren" (literally, "shang" and "person"), initially referred to

to unite chiefdoms and states, gradually weakening the Xia dynasty and eventually destroying it around 1600 BC to establish its own dynasty.

Archaeological excavations have also revealed other large-scale city sites from the Shang dynasty. By around 1300 BC, with the relocation of King Pan'geng to Yin, the Shang ushered in a period of unprecedented prosperity. Yin, as the central city of the late Shang period, continued to thrive until its collapse.

The Shang dynasty lasted for over 550 years before it was overthrown by the Zhou, a state that originated from an ancient tribe in the

Fig. 12 Mao Gong Ding. Please refer to page 23 for more information.

them due to their proficiency in exchange and trade. However, this may be simply wild speculation. Recent studies suggest that the Chinese character "shang" originally refers to an ancient Chinese musical instrument, symbolizing the solemn sound in a temple.

During their nomadic migrations, the Shang people interacted with other tribes, sometimes cooperating and sometimes engaging in conflict. Due to the possibly more dispersed tribal powers in the eastern regions and the possibility of more intense conflicts, the Shang people may have placed greater emphasis on military force. In oracle bone scripts, characters describing violence, conquest, and killing are the most common.

Historical records indicate that by the late Xia dynasty, the Shang had become a powerful state in eastern China, being able

central Shaanxi and the eastern Gansu on the northwestern Loess Plateau. While the Shang dynasty flourished in Yin in present-day Anyang, the Zhou developed into a powerful state and its ruler received the feudal title from the Shang dynasty as a border lord. At the same time, the Zhou people migrated southward to an area later called "Zhouyuan," where they built cities and cultivated fields, making it the birthplace of Zhou culture and the settlement of the Zhou people before it defeated the Shang. The Zhouyuan Site is in today's Fufeng and Qishan counties in Baoji, Shaanxi Province, covering an area as large as Yinxu. It was in the late Qing dynasty that bronze vessels such as the Da Yu Ding (cooking vessel), Da Feng Gui (food vessel), and Mao Gong Ding were unearthed here (see fig. 10 on page 22 and fig. 12).

The Zhou tribe placed significant emphasis on agricultural production, and legend has it that they were descendants of an agricultural deity. Unlike the Shang people who enjoyed drinking, the Zhou people maintained a relatively simple and traditional lifestyle. After relocating to Qishan, the Zhou gradually grew stronger. They successively repelled threats from nomadic tribes in the northwest and consolidated their rule over the middle reach of the Wei River. While focusing on its domestic affairs, the Zhou further united various states and tribes, expanding its influence to the east, ultimately accomplishing the task of "overthrowing the Shang."

Both literature and archaeology coincidentally demonstrate the long history and strong social foundation of the Shang and Zhou dynasties. Excavations of sites such as Yinxu and Zhouyuan provide us with vivid impressions of the two periods. What era was the Shang-Zhou period? What changes occurred from the Shang to the Zhou dynasty?

Shang: A Dark Age

The Shang dynasty was an extremely superstitious era in Chinese history. Not only were sacrifices frequent and extensive, but divination was also prevalent. For matters big or small, such as military expeditions, hunting, or illnesses, the royal family and nobility would consult divination to inquire about auspiciousness or misfortune. The results of the divinations were inscribed onto turtle shells or animal bones in written characters, forming records of various lengths known as oracle inscriptions. These inscriptions, recorded in what is known as "oracle bone scripts," hold significant value for studying the history of the Shang period. The Shang people believed in ghosts and spirits, centering their state politics and social life around them, guided by the concept of the

Mandate of Heaven to determine everything. Human sacrifices served dual purposes: to offer sacrifices to spirits and ancestors for blessings, and to demonstrate that their power came from their ancestors and the heavens, thereby legitimizing their authority through rituals. The distinct political feature of the Shang dynasty was the fusion of divine authority with royal authority, known as the unity of ritual and politics, where the Shang ruler served both as a political leader and the head of the group of shamans.

I. Bronze Ware

Besides oracle inscriptions, bronze ware is frequently seen among the unearthed artifacts from the Shang dynasty. The bronze culture in the period is renowned for its variety and intricacy. While bronze wares were used in daily life and for religious, political, business, and military purposes, the most well-known were ritual vessels. These vessels were for Shang rulers and nobles to host banquets, ceremonies, and other events of ceremonial purposes, including food containers, wine vessels, or water containers and serving as symbols of status, wealth, and power. Constituting the majority of bronze wares, bronze ritual vessels unearthed from Shang dynasty sites total several thousand. Bronze ritual vessels were used to offer food and drinks to gods and ancestors, to communicate with them and to seek their protection and guidance. The importance of bronze ritual vessels in religious and ceremonial rites can also be seen from Shang tombs, where bronze ritual vessels were buried alongside the deceased to accompany them into the afterlife and provide for their needs in the next life. One such vessel used in sacrificial activities is the bronze yan vessel (an ancient boiler) containing the skull of a young girl (fig. 13).

Shang dynasty bronze wares are often large in size and structurally complex. The production of such objects required substantial resources and skilled labor. Without a powerful state apparatus, it would have been impossible to produce them. Furthermore, Shang dynasty bronze wares were renowned for their exquisite beauty and intricate decorations. These elaborate designs often carried profound symbolic meanings, reflecting the beliefs, values, and culture of the Shang people. One of the most common motifs found on Shang dynasty bronze wares is the taotie, a stylized animal face also known as the "beast-mask patterns." It is often depicted as either devouring something or being devoured by other taotie. It represents one of the finest achievements in the decoration of bronze wares, symbolizing the highest level of craftsmanship in bronze ware decoration. The taotie may be seen as a protective deity, and its use on bronze wares may have been intended to provide spiritual protection to those who used them. Additionally, because the taotie has only a large head and a big mouth, it is extremely greedy, eating whatever it encounters. Due to its excessive eating, it is ultimately believed to have died from overeating, hence it is also considered a symbol of greed in later generations (fig. 14).

Fig. 13   Bronze Yan Vessel
Shang dynasty
Height 30.7 cm, diameter at mouth 22.4 cm
Yinxu Museum, Anyang, Henan Province

This bronze vessel was unearthed from a sacrificial pit at Yinxu, Anyang, Henan Province. A yan is an ancient cooking utensil, with the upper part used to hold food and the lower part to contain water, similar to a modern steamer. Surprisingly, a human skull was found inside this yan. Through analysis of the skull, scholars confirmed that it belonged to a girl approximately 15 years old. She was likely a war captive used in human sacrifice and was eventually placed in the tomb as a burial accompaniment.

Fig. 14   A Taotie Motif on an Early Shang Dynasty Bronze Zun

The taotie is a ferocious beast from ancient Chinese mythology. Bronze vessels from the Shang and Zhou periods often feature animal face designs such as the taotie, reflecting a reverence for gods at the time. Shamans would use the patterns to communicate with deities, adding a sense of mystique. Additionally, the fearsome animal face motifs symbolize the authority of royal power, instilling awe and fear in those who beheld them.

Fig. 15   Bronze Sacred Tree

Shang dynasty
Height 396 cm, diameter at
base 93.5 cm
Sanxingdui Museum, Deyang,
Sichuan Province

This bronze artifact is
considered the largest
discovered in China
to date. The base has
three connected legs,
symbolizing the three
mythical mountains of
Penglai, Fangzhang, and
Yingzhou in Chinese
mythology. The tree is
cast in the base center and
divided into three layers,
each with three branches,
totaling nine branches. It is
believed to be a sacred tree,
possibly serving as a ladder
for the ancient people to
connect with the gods and
the heavens.

2. Mysterious Sanxingdui

As the core region of Shang dynasty rule, the primary sites where bronze ritual vessels have been unearthed have long been concentrated in the Central Plains region. However, in the 1980s, a large number of exquisitely crafted bronze artifacts with unique designs were unearthed in sacrificial pits at the Sanxingdui site in Guanghan City, Sichuan Province in southwestern China, showing the highly developed bronze culture in the Yangtze River basin. Among the most remarkable discoveries are bronze figurines. The most striking finds were three large bronze masks (fig. 16) represented with angular human features of protruding almond-shaped eyes and exaggeratedly elongated ears. The massive Bronze Sacred Tree (fig. 15) unearthed is even more extraordinarily unique, possibly related to the religious beliefs of the time. The discovery of the Sanxingdui site confirms the existence of the ancient Shu

Fig. 16 Bronze Beast Mask
Shang dynasty
Length 138 cm, width 85 cm, height 66 cm
Sanxingdui Museum, Deyang, Sichuan Province

This bronze mask is the most uniquely shaped among the many masks unearthed at Sanxingdui. The eyes are slanted and elongated, with the brows sharply raised and cylindrical eyeballs protruding forward up to 16 cm. The ears are fully extended to both sides. The mouth is wide and deep, forming a mysterious smile. It resembles the Clairvoyant and Clairaudient figures from Chinese mythology.

civilization in southwestern China three to four thousand years ago. Its peak period was likely during the Shang dynasty, when it was an important vassal state. However, with the fall of the Shang, the Sanxingdui civilization suddenly disappeared. While there are still many mysteries surrounding the relationship between the Sanxingdui bronze culture in the southwestern Sichuan and the bronze culture of the Shang dynasty in the Central Plains waiting to be unraveled, the profound and mysterious religious features shared between them remain consistent.

From a present-day perspective, it may be difficult to comprehend why the large-scale rituals were frequently held with enormous quantities of human sacrifices and exquisite and mysterious bronze ritual vessels. However, for the people of that time, these practices might have been effective means to unite people, strengthen royal authority, and promote social progress. This is why the period under the rule of King Wuding, during which the Shang dynasty witnessed the highest number of human sacrifices after relocating to Yin, is considered by historians as the peak of the dynasty. In conclusion, the culture of the Shang dynasty is vastly different from today's Chinese perception of life. Despite its brutality and frightfulness, it remains unavoidable as a "dark age." As part of the process of Chinese civilization, only by confronting it can we see through its darkness and welcome the impending light.

The Duke of Zhou

Early Chinese historical texts often depict the last ruler of a dynasty as a "tyrant," who is blamed for the downfall of his dynasty. King Zhou, the last ruler of the Shang dynasty, is one of the typical examples. However, archaeological discoveries and close examination of the literature suggest that King Zhou was more likely a failed reformer. He seemed to attempt reforms in the religious system, reducing human and animal sacrifices, which later generations criticized as neglecting proper rituals. He also mishandled relations with his relatives and nobles, appointing individuals of low status. However, these might simply reflect a more humane approach to life. His most significant failure might have been prioritizing the suppression of rebellion in the east, neglecting the rising power of the Zhou in the west. Ultimately, he was decisively defeated by the army led by King Wu of Zhou in the Battle of Muye near the capital. He then

chose to immolate himself, in a desperate act of dedicating himself to the gods and his ancestors, realizing the highest level of sacrifice for his empire.

1. Overthrowing the Shang

King Wu of Zhou, who defeated King Zhou, and his father, King Wen of Zhou, who laid the foundation for their military success, were not the most prominent figures during the transition from the Shang to the Zhou. The person who truly revitalized the Zhou dynasty was King Wu's brother, Duke of Zhou. Two years after the establishment of the Zhou dynasty, King Wu passed away, leaving his young son under the guardianship of the Duke of Zhou to manage the newly established state. After King Wu defeated Shang's army, he enfeoffed King Zhou of Shang's son, Wu Geng, in Yin and sent his three brothers to supervise him. Considering King Wu's death a window of opportunity to restore their lost dynasty, some remnants of Shang with Wu Geng as the head, along with the three brothers of King Wu, incited the tribes in east China to launch a large-scale rebellion against the newly established dynasty. It was the Duke of Zhou who led troops from the Zhou capital in present-day Xi'an, Shaanxi Province, to march eastward against the rebels. After three years of brutal warfare, the rebellion was quelled, and the eastern tribes were subdued, extending Zhou's influence to the lower Yellow River basin and the Huai River basin. The scale and ferocity of the conflicts far exceeded that of King Wu's battle against the Shang, and its significance was much greater. After suppressing the rebellion led by Wu Geng, the Duke of Zhou relocated Shang people to the north bank of the Luo River and ordered them to build a new capital city. This city, later known as Luoyang, became an important political and military hub to conquer the whole region of East China. As a result, the two well-known ancient capitals in China, Chang'an and Luoyang, began to take shape. They served as the two major ruling centers of the Zhou dynasty, connecting east and west of China for more than five hundred kilometers, forming the foundation of a mighty empire.

2. Enfeoffment of Vassals

Alongside the construction of the Eastern Capital (i.e., Luoyang), another significant initiative during the early years of the Zhou dynasty was the extensive enfeoffment (granting of land or titles in return for service) of the vassals. Initially, most of the vassals enfeoffed were relatives who shared a surname, but there were also vassals from different surnames, such as descendants of the meritorious warriors who contributed to the downfall of the Shang and the leaders of former states. These vassals had obligations to the royal court, including defending the territory, protecting the royal family, paying tribute, and reporting performance. They were also required to be ready to lead their warriors and armies to participate in warfare following the King's orders. The vassals had the authority to grant land and people within their fiefdoms to their family members and trusted associates, who in turn had obligations of military service and tribute payment to them.

While the practice of enfeoffment existed during the Shang dynasty, it was mainly nominal titles granted to naturally formed states and tribes, lacking a rigorous system and effective control measures, resulting in frequent rebellion among those enfeoffed. In contrast, the enfeoffment system of the Zhou dynasty was more comprehensive as it was based on its active military expansion. This significantly strengthened the royal court's control over the national territory, consolidating the position of the King as the ruler of the empire.

3. Establishing Rituals and Music

The complicated enfeoffment system constituted the hierarchical system and subordinate relationship centered around the Zhou ruler. Nobles were divided into many levels based on the closeness of blood ties, managing their clansmen based on kinship. Its core was the system of primogeniture. How was the social structure maintained? It required a series of rules and regulations from political, cultural, and other aspects, with the core being a set of etiquette systems distinguishing between closeness and distance, high and low, and superior and subordinate, each accompanied by corresponding music and dance. The system of rituals and music was not invented out of thin air at the beginning, but was further perfected and developed into a typical and systematic structure, with the Duke of Zhou playing a key role. "Establishing rituals and music" is believed to be one of the most significant achievements of the Duke's life.

Once established, the ritual and music system was widely applied in various aspects of politics and society, defining each individual's position in the social order and coordinating the relationships among members of a community. This is the basic spirit of the Zhou's etiquette system. The focus of the rituals and music system was on humans rather than gods. The Zhou people revered heaven and spirits, but they placed more emphasis on human affairs. The fundamental purpose of governing the empire, as advocated by the rulers, was to nurture the people. With the curtain falling on gods and spirits and the sound of etiquette and music ringing out, the most dramatic political and cultural reform in Chinese history was put into practice (see fig. 17 on pages 32–33).

The Duke of Zhou, who initiated the reforms, returned the royal authority to his nephew after his seven-year regency, without becoming the sovereign of the dynasty. However, what he achieved in consolidating the unity of the dynasty and establishing imperial systems surpassed all the monarchs of his empire, elevating his status in the history of the Zhou dynasty and even the entirety of China. As can be expected, he was widely revered for his courage and leadership by Confucian scholars in later generations and honored with the title of "sage."

Competing Major Powers

The Zhou dynasty is the longest-lasting dynasty in Chinese history, spanning nearly 800 years. It is commonly divided into two periods by historians: the Western Zhou (1046–771 BC), as its capital in present-day Xi'an, Shaanxi Province, and the Eastern Zhou (770–256 BC), after the capital moved eastward to Luoyang, in present-day Henan Province. The direct cause of the downfall of the Western Zhou was the domestic conflicts of its last ruler, King You. However, the underlying reason was the weakening power of the state, coincident with the gradual rise of northwest tribes near the central region under the direct rule of the King of Zhou. To avoid incursions from these tribes, the Zhou had to relocate to the eastern capital under the escort of some vassal states, abandoning the old capital area in Shaanxi, around 770 BC. The first half of the Eastern Zhou period is commonly referred to as the Spring and Autumn period (770–476 BC), lasting for about 300 years, followed by the latter half known as the Warring States period.

The Eastern Zhou was markedly different from the Western Zhou in that its royal authority was seriously challenged. The territory under its direct control was limited to no more than a few hundred miles around its capital. The regular tributes from the vassal states could no longer be ensured, leading to severe financial constraints for the

Fig. 17 Chime Bells of Wangsun Gao

Spring and Autumn period (770–476 BC)
Weight 2.8 kg (smallest) to 152.8 kg (biggest)
Henan Museum

This set of chime bells consists of 26 pieces, identical in design but decreasing in size. They were cast by Wangsun Gao, a nobleman from the State of Chu, for his father as a ceremonial musical instrument, reflecting the majesty of the Chu royal family. This set is currently the largest, most extensive, widest-ranging in pitch, most accurately tuned, and best-preserved set of bronze percussion instruments from the Spring and Autumn period.

royal court. More importantly, the traditional social and political order was being destroyed, and the hierarchical system was seriously undermined. In surprising breaks with conventions, even ceremonies and rituals began to be held by individual vassal states, rather than the royal court, as they had been.

So, what was the landscape of the vassal states in the Eastern Zhou dynasty? A large number of vassal states were enfeoffed during the Western Zhou period. According to historical records, more than 120 remained till the Spring and Autumn period. These so-called vassal states were initially isolated areas of cultivation, with sparse populations and concentrated settlements. Between them, there were often large areas of open space. A "state" was often no more than a "city-state," resulting in the overall structure of the Zhou dynasty resembling a dotted pattern. Through the distribution of these city centers, the Zhou dynasty radiated Huaxia civilization to its whole territory. As can be imagined, due to the large gaps in between, there was little contact between states, let alone conflict or war. However, as the royal authority declined, connections between states were strengthened due to the economic and cultural advancement of individual vassal states and the improvement of transportation. Territories began to connect, leading to more frequent wars. As a result, the Eastern Zhou period was not only an era in Chinese history marked by numerous city-states but also diverse diplomacy because of its frequent warfare. It left behind many well-known stories, and many of the idioms and stories learned by Chinese children today from an early age are derived from the Eastern Zhou period.

So, what are the differences between the Spring and Autumn and the Warring States periods? The history of the former can be described as a history of hegemony among major states. The vassal states were in constant warfare and the Zhou dynasty was effectively fragmented. However, the nominal status and influence of the Zhou king as the ruler had not vanished. Military actions among major states and their commands and annexations of smaller states all required the pretext of "royal decree." Another excuse was "resisting foreign invasions."

The name Huaxia first appeared during the Western Zhou dynasty, becoming a general term for the inhabitants of the Central Plains. Generally, those vassals and subjects enfeoffed by the Zhou royal family considered themselves as part of the Huaxia group, distinguishing themselves from neighboring, relatively backward ethnic groups. From the Western Zhou to the Spring and Autumn period, the influence of the "foreign states around the Central Plains" increased, further expanding into the core Central Plains region of the Huaxia. They either lived together on frontiers mixing with people of the Huaxia states or filled the vacant lands between states, posing a significant threat to the Huaxia states. For example, the Zhou was forced to relocate its capital east solely due to the military pressure from the Quanrong tribe beyond its northwestern border. During the Eastern Zhou period, the powerful state of Chu, located in the middle Yangtze River basin, posed the greatest threat to the Huaxia. The ruler of Chu traditionally called himself "king," but it was not one of the vassals enfeoffed by the Zhou dynasty. From a certain perspective, it can be said that the conflicts between the two major Central Plains states—Qi in Shandong and Jin in Shanxi—and Chu, the most powerful state among the "foreign states around the Central Plains," dominated the warfare of the Spring and Autumn period. In addition, even the major state of Qin in western China was considered part of the Huaxia only in comparison with the "foreign states" beyond their western borders. It was initially enfeoffed as a lower-ranking vassal for providing horses for the Zhou royal family. After Zhou relocated its capital to Luoyang, Qin's mixed residency with other non-Huaxia people continued to increase and conflicts between them intensified; as such, it was regarded as culturally inferior by other major states in the Central Plains. Qin rose during the Spring and Autumn period through constant conflicts with its northwestern neighbors, ultimately expanding its territory and even occupying territories formerly belonging to the Zhou. Finally, Wu and Yue, dominant powers in the late Spring and Autumn period, were both states in the Taihu Lake region in the lower Yangtze River basin and were not originally members of the Huaxia group.

Between the Huaxia and the "foreign states," there were also peaceful communications. For example, numerous records are documented regarding intermarriage between them. Through centuries of interaction, the two sides continued to merge. By the transition from the Spring and Autumn to the Warring States period, most of the ethnic groups entering the Central Plains had already assimilated into the Huaxia. States like Chu and Qin were no longer seen as foreign states.

Fig. 18 Chariots on bronze mirrors with hunting motifs from the Warring States period (475–221 BC).

Eventually, after the unification of China by the Qin dynasty (221–206 BC), a unified and enduring Han ethnic group emerged.

The three hundred years of warfare among the states dramatically reduced the number of small states. By the time of the Warring States period, only about a dozen states remained, the most significant being Qin, Chu, Yan, and Qi, as well as Han, Zhao, and Wei, which split from the original major state of Jin during the Spring and Autumn period. These seven major states were collectively known as the "Seven Warring States." The wars during the Spring and Autumn period primarily focused on seizing border territories and conquering small states, carried out with the refined characteristic of aristocrats, mainly involving chariot warfare and smaller-scale conflicts. In contrast, the wars of the Warring States period aimed at annihilating the enemy's main forces, with infantry as the primary force and cavalry as support. Moreover, becoming a soldier was no longer limited to aristocrats, as conscription was widely practiced across states, leading to a significant increase in military numbers and the scale and lethality of warfare far surpassing that of the Spring and Autumn period. This is why this era is known as the "Warring States" period (fig. 18). It was during this time that the world's earliest military treatise, *The Art of War* by Chinese military general, strategist, philosopher, and writer Sun Zi (also Sun Tzu), along with numerous other military works, was written, highlighting the advanced state of military science.

Scholars and Schools of Thought

In addition to economic growth, there were significant changes in the social structure during the Warring States period. The hierarchical system was further disrupted as political reforms were introduced in the major states, gradually establishing a bureaucratic

Fig. 19 A Portrait of Confucius

Ma Yuan (1140–1227)
Ink and color on silk
Length 23.1 cm, height 27.7 cm
The Palace Museum, Beijing

In this painting, Confucius is depicted wearing a long robe, standing with his hands clasped, exuding a calm and solemn demeanor with a vivid expression. The lines are powerful and expressive, capturing his form and spirit with just a few strokes.

system under monarchic autocracy. The feudal system based on clan hierarchy and land allocation began to disintegrate. Officials at all levels, from the central government to local administrations, were appointed and dismissed by the monarch based on merit rather than favoritism. A new class of intellectuals, known as "scholars" (shi), emerged in the social structure. Originally, the term referred to adult males from the lower nobility. They held noble status, were granted a certain amount of land, and received traditional aristocratic education. In peacetime, they served as retainers for monarchs or senior nobles, and in times of wars, they became soldiers. By the Spring and Autumn period, especially during the Warring States era, academia and classics, previously monopolized by the aristocracy, began to spread to the lower strata of society. This led to the rise of grassroots intellectual gatherings, and Confucius in the late Spring and Autumn period was a representative in this movement.

In such a context, by the Warring States period, the meaning of "scholar" continued to change. It became detached from one's lineage, identified as someone learned and talented. The training of scholars had shifted from a focus on both military and literary skills to primarily studying cultural classics. Unconstrained by the hierarchical system, they could freely move between states. What they learned was no longer limited by social status or personal interests but rather driven by pragmatic political considerations. This shift aligned with the development of the bureaucratic system and became a prevalent characteristic of ancient Chinese scholars for a subsequent 2000 years.

The Warring States period was among the most active periods for scholars in Chinese history, giving rise to numerous theories and schools of thought, many of which had profoundly important influences on the future of China.

1. Confucius

Confucius (551–479 BC), the founder of Confucianism (fig. 19), was not only the first philosopher in Chinese history, but also one of the earliest philosophers in human history. He was born in the state of Lu during the Spring and Autumn period. His ancestors were nobles from the state of Song, but by the time of his birth, his family had fallen on hard times. Nevertheless, as a child, he received a good aristocratic education. Confucius formulated his own theories about ethical, moral, and socio-political issues in the context of the turbulent Spring and Autumn period, thus establishing the renowned Confucian school of thought. However, Confucius achieved no significant political success during his time, as his political ideas were not accepted by the vassals of the era. Where he truly excelled was in the field of education. As a pioneer of private teaching in China, he imparted his academic and political ideas to the students he widely recruited. It is believed that Confucius had 3,000 disciples, among whom 72 were outstanding. It was these students, as well as their students, who inherited and developed his thoughts after his death. Through travels across various states, they promoted political reforms, spread Confucian teachings, and disseminated classical literature (see fig. 20 on the next page).

2. Mencius and Xunzi

By the time of the Warring States period, Confucianism, founded by Confucius, had evolved into several branches, the most prominent being those of Mencius (372–289 BC) and Xunzi (c. 313–238 BC). The former emphasized Confucius' doctrine of "benevolence," advocating for reducing punishment, lightening taxes, and opposing violence, believing that by doing so, one could become invincible and achieve the goal of unifying China. Mencius' teachings

Fig. 20 Confucius Temples are temple buildings constructed to commemorate Confucius, and they are present in many cities across China. The Confucius Temple in Qufu, Shandong Province, is the largest temple complex in China.

leaned towards populism, asserting that "the people are the most important, the state is next, and the ruler is the least." Mencius was revered by later Confucian scholars as second only to Confucius, known as the "Second Sage." Xunzi, on the other hand, emphasized monarchical centralized power and unity, believing that governing a state relied heavily on ritual and education, but also acknowledging the necessity of laws and punishments. He also emphasized the transformation of nature through human efforts and the utilization of natural laws. The fundamental difference between Mencius and Xunzi lies in Mencius' belief in the innate goodness of human nature while Xunzi stressed the innate evilness of human nature. Despite facing criticism from some orthodox Confucians in later generations, Xunzi's thoughts became the governing principles of later autocratic dynasties in ancient China. As proponents who further developed Confucianism during the Warring States period, Mencius and Xunzi advanced Confucian teachings significantly in terms of personal cultivation and political philosophy, making Confucianism the most prominent school of thought at that time. From the Western Han dynasty (202 BC–AD 8) onwards, Confucianism became the official ideology of China, deeply influencing the collective psychology and national character of the Chinese people, an influence that persists to this day.

3. Taoists

Another school of thought that had a profound impact on future China is Taoism (or Daoism), represented by Laozi and Zhuangzi. They proposed an important philosophical concept "Tao," believing it to be an intangible but transcendent existence beyond time and space, the origin of all things in the world. Intangible and unknowable as it is, Tao is an absolute spirit. Then, do we as humans need to actively transform the world and society? In contrast to the proactive Confucian approach, Taoism advocates passivity and detachment from the world. It emphasizes both the restoration of natural human instincts at a personal level and governing a state through non-action, aiming for a populace devoid of desires and knowledge. Taoism was not the most prominent school of thought during the Warring States period, but its significant influence on later China stems from its role as a spiritual refuge for individuals, particularly scholars who sought solace amidst the chaos of war, career setbacks, and shattered personal aspirations. Especially during the Han dynasty's decline, when Taoism as a religion emerged with the influence of Taoist philosophy, its impact on the Chinese psyche became even more profound, a topic that will be discussed in subsequent chapters.

4. Legalists

During the Warring States period, especially towards its end, the Legalist school was a particularly noteworthy faction among the diverse schools of thought. As the period progressed, the small-scale societies based on the feudal system of clan hierarchy and land allocation gradually evolved into larger and more complex entities. With intensifying conflicts and wars of annexation, the states sought to improve governance efficiency and alter the landscape of aristocratic power struggles from the late Spring and Autumn period. They did so by implementing authoritarian centralization and initiating legal reforms. The reform movements were largely guided by Legalist ideologies. Characterized by the prioritization of sovereign authority and the promotion of rule by law, Legalism adapted to the historical trend of bureaucratic centralization replacing the feudal system. It also aligned with the demands of militarization and agricultural emphasis amidst the backdrop of wars of annexation. Among the reform efforts, the most thorough and impactful was the Legalist-inspired reform spearheaded by the statesman, chancellor and reformer Shang Yang in the state of Qin. The state-wide implementation of Legalist principles profoundly influenced its governance practices and eventually contributed significantly to the establishment of the Qin dynasty.

The Warring States period ended in 221 BC, when the state of Qin, which had a history of over 500 years, conquered the last remaining major state, Qi, marking the birth of the first unified empire in Chinese history under an absolute monarchy. As the result of the long-term efforts of its rulers and people, Qin stood out among over a hundred vassal states that co-existed in the Eastern Zhou period and prospered through prolonged confrontations with northwestern nomadic tribes. Eventually, it defeated six other states in about a decade. With this, the most turbulent era in Chinese history came to an end. However, amid the turmoil, schools of thought proliferated and differing views were expressed. At the same time, ancient people began to break free from the shackles of primitive witchcraft and religious beliefs, laying the foundation for a more rational spirit based on rituals and music, accomplishments, and achievements. It was in this lengthy process that an advanced Chinese empire gradually took shape and developed.

CHAPTER THREE
The Human World: Qin and Han Dynasties

Around 1.5 kilometers east of the mausoleum of the first Chinese emperor, Qin Shihuang (259–210 BC), in Lintong, Xi'an City, Shaanxi Province, is the Emperor Qinshihuang's Mausoleum Site Museum. It houses the most significant archaeological excavations of the 20th century—a large collection of terracotta sculptures depicting the emperor's imperial guard troops in the form of funerary art buried with him, with the purpose of protecting his tomb and accompanying him into the afterlife. The figures, dating from approximately the late 3rd century BC, are life-sized and vary in posture, facial expression, and armor and weaponry in accordance with rank. The painted surface present on them began to flake and fade soon after excavation, but the massive earth-toned assembly in battle formations and the incredible feat of craftsmanship and production leave every visitor in awe.

What tourists see today, however, is only the front and fragmentary part of a much larger mausoleum, leaving them to wonder how majestic the mysterious Qin Shihuang's Mausoleum, which has not yet been fully

excavated for technical reasons, will be behind these terracotta warriors and horses. Qin Shihuang conquered much in his lifetime, but his driving purpose was even greater; he sought to construct a microcosm of his imperial palace and his formidable army— warriors, infantrymen, horses, chariots and all their attendant armor and weaponry, which helped him merge the six rival states into one nation through wars. Driven to conquer death itself, the first emperor left behind a treasure to be discovered to show how ambitious but pragmatic the newly established social order in a unified imperial China was (fig. 21).

On the facing page and the right

Fig. 21 Warrior figurines in Pit No.1 of the Emperor Qin Shihuang's Terracotta Army Museum. Currently, three pits have been discovered, estimated to contain approximately 7,000 warrior figurines, 100 chariots, and 100 horses based on the current arrangement of the terracotta warriors. These pottery figurines are tall, generally around 1.8 meters in height.

An Empire Administered by Documents

Qin Shihuang realized that a fragmented culture and diverse traditions could pose significant challenges to centralized governance. After unifying the country in 221 BC, he gave priority to the tasks of standardizing the law, weights, measures (fig. 22), coinage, writing and chariot axle width to facilitate trade, communication and road transportation among people who had belonged to culturally and economically differing rival states. New standards were not prescribed by synthesizing the systems of various states but instead, practices in the former Qin were forcefully promoted. As a matter of fact, the reform measures could hardly have significant impact on the daily lives of ordinary people, who could not care less about writing, axle width, and weights and measures. Those craftsmen and officials who had to work according to new specifications and regulations were the main implementers of the reforms.

To better govern the vast territory, the emperor ordered the construction of an extensive network of roads with the capital Xianyang (present-day Xianyang in Shaanxi Province) as the transportation hub. Added to the long-distance traffic arteries leading far east, north, and southeast were more regional networks of well-connected roads. More importantly, the extensive wall fortifications built by the former rival states of Qin, Zhao and Yan as protection against marauding nomadic groups were joined as today's famous Great Wall to position the empire against the Xiongnu people from the north (figs. 23–25 on pages 43 to 45).

Qin Shihuang abolished the enfeoffment

Fig. 22 Box-Shaped Sheng (Measuring Vessel) Cast in Bronze, Invented by Shang Yang

Qin state, Warring States period
Length 18.7 cm, width 6.9 cm, depth 2.3 cm, volume 202.15 ml
Shanghai Museum

This was a standard measuring vessel used for calculating volume, with inscriptions indicating it was manufactured under the supervision of Shang Yang. This slightly larger-than-hand-sized bronze artifact bears witness to the implementation of Qin standards across the empire after Qin Shihuang unified China for the first time in Chinese history, which led to the establishment of the territorial, institutional, and cultural foundations of Chinese civilization for millennia to come.

system that was based on consanguinity, which had been in place since the Western Zhou period. Instead, a vertical government system of prefectures and counties was established. Under the new system, local officials were appointed, and their performance was evaluated by the central government. The rule of the Qin dynasty extended progressively from the imperial court down to the local level, exerting state control at each tier. National authority, flowing from the top to the bottom, reached the lowest levels of society and, conversely, concentrated from the bottom to the top, ultimately culminating in the hands of the emperor. As a result, officials at each level responsible to the central government replaced the former regional lords who assumed full authority over their own territory and people. The new ruling paradigm was adopted as the fundamental governance model by all later dynasties.

Fig. 23 Qin dynasty (221–206 BC) Great Wall in Guyang, Baotou, Inner Mongolia Autonomous Region.

Fig. 24 The Han Great Wall Ruins in Dunhuang, Jiuquan, Gansu Province.

Figs. 23–25 Sections of the Great Wall were built and rebuilt in the Qin, Han (202 BC–AD 8), and Ming dynasties. Most of the Great Wall that we see today was constructed during the Ming dynasty (1368–1644). With continuous repairs and expansions over dynasties, the total length of the Great Wall in Chinese history has reached 21,196.18 kilometers.

Fig. 25 Jinshanling Great Wall in Hebei Province, an essential section of the Ming dynasty Great Wall.

1. Writing on Bamboo and Wooden Slips

The Qin dynasty lasted only fifteen years, from 221 to 206 BC, making it the shortest-lived dynasty among the unified dynasties in Chinese history. In contrast, the Han dynasty, which followed Qin, endured for more than 400 years, becoming an exemplary dynasty of the imperial era. The Qin emperor is known for his "autocratic rule," which is also the principal reason for the dynasty's collapse. Among his tyrannical policies were military priority, severe laws, and absolute authority, while the well-being of the people was neglected. However, the Han attempted to recuperate and build up strength after the harsh rule of the Qin: reducing the tax rate on households' agricultural produce, doing away with legal punishments involving mutilation, declaring widespread amnesties, and switching to a more cautious approach to foreign policy. Added to the new policies was its effective administrative system to govern the vast empire, known as "administration by written documents," which was likely first promoted in the Qin dynasty.

According to the historical text *Shiji* (*Records of the Grand Historian*) by historian Sima Qian of the Han dynasty, Qin Shihuang spent most of his time reviewing briefing reports from the court departments and local officials, making final decisions on all important political affairs. The autocratic and hands-on emperor used scales to measure how many documents he had examined. What he read were messages written on narrow strips of wood or bamboo, each typically holding a single column of several dozen brush-written characters. For longer texts, slips were sewn together with hemp, silk, or leather to make them into a folding book, called jiandu. Bamboo and wooden slips were the main media for writing documents in China before the widespread introduction of paper. They might have been invented earlier in Chinese writing history, but the earliest surviving examples date from the Warring States period. Bamboo or wooden strips were the standard writing material for hundreds of years from Qin through Han to Eastern Jin (317–420) before they were gradually displaced by the invention of paper from mainstream uses. By the end of Eastern Jin at the turn of the 5th century AD, jiandu was largely abandoned as a medium for writing in China.

Thanks to the discovery of ancient bamboo slips in northwestern China in the early 20th century and the recent large-scale excavation of bamboo slips, particularly in Hunan and Hubei provinces (respectively in south-central and central China), what the documents in the Qin and Han periods look like and how officials administered, both centrally and locally, through written reports are known to the public. The texts on bamboo slips mainly include subjects of military affairs, judiciary matters, account books, and household registers. They have been discovered not only in military and administrative sites but also in private tombs, where they were buried along with divination records, medical prescriptions, traditional Chinese almanacs, and other practical documents.

Research into the ancient bamboo and wooden slips has revealed the administrative procedures under which the vast country was ruled: an imperial edict from the emperor was distributed to local governments throughout the country. Because bamboo slips can be sewn together, each office attached their written response slips to the original and passed it down to an office at a lower level. Alternatively, a request document would be submitted to upper-level governments and comment slips were added until it reaches the imperial court. As additional slips could be attached, each level of office shows whether the decree is executed or not by adding executive texts and signature. In other words, the content, format, shape, and writing material of the

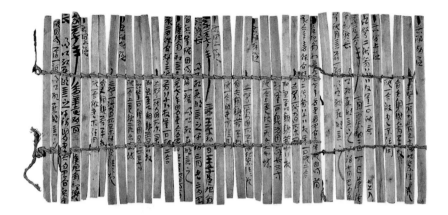

Fig. 26   A Section of *Yongyuan Inventory*

This is one of the most perfectly conserved register documents from the Han dynasty bamboo slips. Recorded by a frontier official at the time, it shows the storage status of weapons in the frontier armory. The records are very detailed about loans, damages, or purchases, to ensure accurate handover to the incoming defenders.

bamboo slips, along with the way they were disseminated, constitute an emperor's power and demonstrates the effective exercise of his authority (fig. 26).

In the 1990s, a collection of ancient Chinese bamboo manuscripts was discovered in tombs at the Shuihudi archaeological site in Yunmeng County, Hubei Province. The texts record Qin laws and public documents. Among them are legal provisions applied before the Qin unified China. They stipulate that reports on government affairs must be submitted in written form and that oral communication is prohibited, indicating that "administration by written documents" had been well in place. The projects of unifying the script and improving the road system, therefore, helped in standardizing official documents and improving their transmission. This was essential to ensure the functioning and efficiency of the imperial state with a centralized authority. Consequently, the governance of "administration by written documents" was established as the first imperial state was founded in China.

2. Xi, a Local Official

One of the keys of the administration by written documents lay in the lowest level of imperial administration, in addition to the emperor Qin Shihuang, who sat atop and issued decrees. It was through grassroots officials that the empire's decisions were implemented and the emperor's rule effectively established. Inevitably, the process placed demands on the literacy skills of grassroots officials. After all, in the early days of the imperial era, the literacy rate was far lower than in the present day.

Among the local officials was Xi, the owner of Shuihudi bamboo manuscripts. He was born in the former territory of the Chu state, which had already been occupied by the Qin state before Qin Shihuang unified China. From a young age, he began studying various subjects, including laws and regulations. At the age of 20, he became a local clerk in his village and spent his entire life serving as a grassroots bureaucrat in local villages, counties, and prefectures, responsible for drafting, receiving, and storing official documents. He also adjudicated local criminal cases. Xi was one of the numerous grassroots officials of that era. He participated in the military campaigns of the Qin's conquest of the six other states and saw the emperor himself when he inspected his hometown after the unification. More importantly, he

Fig. 27 Qin Dynasty Slips Titled *The Way of the Official*

Qin dynasty

Length 27.5 cm, totaling 51 slips

Hubei Provincial Museum

These bamboo slips provide detailed documentary evidence reflecting the legal and administrative systems of the Qin dynasty. They also offer a glimpse into the artistry of calligraphy on bamboo slips from that era.

devoted his whole life to the service of the emperor as one of the grassroots implementers in the local government. Among Xi's burial objects is a self-written biography that allows us to understand his life. Other objects include divination documents, legal texts with explanations, criminal cases, and a book on the way of being an official (fig. 27).

The governance of the Qin, from top to bottom, was designed to ensure the smooth and thorough implementation of laws and decrees. With the formidable army as showcased in the terracotta army pits, the functioning of the state system was characterized by its countless grassroots officials proficient in writing and knowledgeable in laws. Subsequently, the Han dynasty inherited this system of administration by written documents. By the early Han period, the training of local officials was formalized, and the legal system based on laws and regulations was further solidified.

Dissident Confucian Scholars

Following the short-lived Qin, the Han dynasty ruled China for centuries, greatly expanding the Chinese empire. The founder of the Han, Liu Bang (c. 256 or 247–195 BC), who reigned from 202 BC to 195 BC, began his career as a minor official under the Qin dynasty. One day on his way escorting a group called up for military service to Xianyang, the capital of the Qin, he saw in the distance Emperor Qin Shihuang on a major expedition, accompanied by a grand procession. Taken aback by how mighty the emperor was sitting on a lavishly decorated carriage, the young Liu Bang couldn't help but exclaim, "A great man should be like this!" Little could anyone imagine that the humble official would establish a greater empire to replace the Qin, leaving a glorious mark in history.

1. Burning Books and Burying Scholars

As we mentioned in Chapter Two, the Qin owed its victories over other states to Legalism as its ideological and talent foundation. While reforming measures were introduced, to various extents, during the late Warring States period in all states, the Qin was known for its most thorough and influential reforms. Legalism, characterized by its reverence for imperial authority and emphasis on rule by law, met heavy military and agricultural demands during times of war. It also aligned with the autocratic rule of a monarch, and Qin Shihuang himself was a monarch deeply influenced by Legalist theories, with a character marked by authoritarianism and suspicion. Legalism holds three "treasures"—law, tactics, and power. Laws are enforced to regulate what individuals can or cannot do, tactics are applied to manipulate one's subordinates, and power represents the authority over laws and tactics.

After the unification of China, Qin Shihuang further implemented Legalist ideology and practices into his rule, as manifested in his empire's exceptionally harsh legal system. His subjects were frequently punished or even executed for violating his strict laws and regulations. In the realm of ideological thought, two significant events occurred—burning books and burying dissident Confucian scholars. The former involved the decree that, apart from state histories, medical texts, divination records, agricultural manuals, and classics—*Shijing* (*Classic of Poetry*), *Shangshu* (*Book of Documents*) and other works by various sages—housed in the central governmental academy, all private collections of Confucian classics, philosophical texts, and other historical works were to be collected and destroyed within a stipulated period. Those discussing the *Classic of Poetry* and the *Book of Documents* were to be executed, while a whole clan was to be exterminated when a member of the family criticized the present by referring to the past. Private schools were strictly prohibited. The latter event occurred in 212 BC when some alchemists and Confucian scholars expressed dissatisfaction with Qin Shihuang, prompting his ire. He ordered the capture of over 460 dissidents, all of whom were subsequently executed and buried in Xianyang, the capital city. These two events inflicted severe damage on Chinese intellectual and cultural heritage, intensifying resentment among intellectuals towards the Qin dynasty. Hence, in the tomb of Xi, all the books buried together with him were related to medicine, divination, or law, in addition to *The Way of the Official*, reflecting the intellectual landscape of the Qin dynasty. "Officials as teachers and law as education" was not only a state policy of the Qin dynasty but also the sole means for intellectuals to acquire knowledge at that time.

2. From Taoism to Confucianism

At the outset of the Han dynasty, its founder Liu Bang held disdain for Confucian scholars. It was through military conquests, he believed, that he had gained control of the empire. At that time, the debater Lu Jia told the new emperor, "One can never govern an empire with force after seizing it by force." This remark by Lu Jia has echoed through the ages, and he later became a distinguished minister of the Han dynasty.

At the inception of the Han dynasty, the primary political measures implemented were those of "resting with the people." This was a political approach formed under the Taoist concept of "governing by non-interference," where the state's basic system was kept as simple as possible, merely following the precedents set by the Qin dynasty without significant alterations. In the realm of ideology, while Legalist theories were no longer universally adopted, alongside the promotion of Taoist thought, other schools of thought also circulated in the society and had officials dedicated to academic research in the court. Among them, the Confucian school, which had long been rooted in society and emphasized textual transmission, classical teachings, and the promotion of ethical morality, had the greatest influence. By the time of Emperor Wu (156–87 BC; reigned 140–87 BC), the Han dynasty had developed into a highly civilized and powerful state. The policy of "non-interference" was no longer applicable, leading to the ascendancy of Confucian scholars and Confucianism itself. This marked the beginning of an era known for its "dismissing hundred schools of thought and revering Confucianism alone," spearheaded by Dong Zhongshu (179–104 BC), one of the most prominent figures in Confucianism at that time (see fig. 28 on the next page).

Just as the Taoist teachings at the beginning of the Han dynasty were not

Fig. 28 *Fu Sheng Expounding the Classic*
Attributed to Wang Wei (701?–761)
Color on silk
Osaka City Museum of Fine Arts

simply a replica of pre-Qin Taoist doctrines, Confucianism at this time was also not entirely identical to that of the pre-Qin period. Dong Zhongshu promoted the hierarchical concepts emphasized by Confucius and Mencius across various social strata. He put forward the "Three Fundamental Bonds" of "lords are superior to their retainers, fathers to their sons, and the husband to his wife," and the "Five Constant Virtues" of "benevolence, righteousness, propriety, wisdom, and trustworthiness" as ethical norms. The core of his ideology was to uphold centralized authority, mythologizing absolute imperial power. Relatedly, after "dismissing the hundred schools of thought," only scholars studying Confucian classics remained in the court's official schools. The talent selection and educational system primarily focused on Confucianism were formulated.

After the book burning and burying of scholars incident under Qin Shihuang, Fu Sheng, a descendant of Confucius's disciple Mi Zijian, fled back to his hometown and risked his life to hide a copy of the *Book of Documents*. When Emperor Wen of Han sought someone knowledgeable in the *Book of Documents*, he discovered Fu Sheng. This painting depicts the elderly Fu Sheng, over 90 years old, orally transmitting the classic to others, preserving it through the ages.

Whether it was the talent selection system of the Han dynasty known as "chaju," where local officials assessed and selected talents within their jurisdiction at any time and recommended them to their superiors or the central government, and appointed them to official positions after trial and evaluation, or the subsequent talent selection systems entering the bureaucratic system through examination systems, particularly after the Tang dynasty (618–907), those selected had to adhere to Confucian ethical standards and be well versed in Confucian classics.

3. Wang Mang's Reign

During the reign of Emperor Wu, the most famous monarch of the Han dynasty, Confucianism and Confucian scholars achieved a revolutionary victory, establishing Confucianism as the official ideology of ancient China. However, its triumph was confined to the realms of academia and ideology. In terms of actual policy-making and personnel appointments, the Han rulers and officials did not strictly adhere to Confucianism alone; rather, they extensively absorbed the administrative thoughts and methods of Legalism, exhibiting a characteristic fusion of the two schools of thought. This ideological feature was also quite typical among Dong Zhongshu and many other Confucian scholars of the Western Han dynasty. Subsequently, Emperor Xuan of Han (92–49 BC, reigned 74–49 BC) summarized this political principle as "employing both hegemony and various schools of thought." However, when Confucian scholars truly sought to ascend to the political forefront and construct a real world based on the ideals of peace depicted in Confucian classics, the shortcomings of Confucian thought in terms of practical governance became apparent, as it lacked both the means and imagination for dealing with real-world affairs. The same scene unfolded during the Han dynasty.

In the late Western Han dynasty, social crises frequently arose, and the monarchy further developed into despotism. At the same time, the maternal and marital clans wielded central power, while Confucianism enjoyed unprecedented dominance in the ideological realm. Wang Mang (45 BC–AD 23), who hailed from one of these clans and was known for being versed in Confucian rites, practicing frugality, and promoting virtuous officials, emerged as a promising candidate for auxiliary governance throughout the court and society. However, despite Wang Mang's political maneuvering to seize power, his fervent Confucianism led him to blindly believe in ancient texts and classics, disregarding practical social and economic laws. While he had intentions and measures to alleviate social crises, his attempts to reform based on Confucian classics and ancient systems often remained theoretical, with numerous flaws and impracticalities in execution. Thus, a figure initially seen as a savior of the society eventually became the scapegoat for the ruling crisis in the later Western Han period. The Xin dynasty (8–23) established by Wang Mang ultimately failed in the face of large-scale peasant uprisings, lasting only 16 years from its inception to the end, similar to the duration of the Qin dynasty. Ban Gu (32–92), a historian of the Eastern Han (25–220), described Wang Mang's extreme superstition in Confucianism as akin to Emperor Qin Shihuang's extreme actions of burning books and burying Confucian scholars, leading to a similar fate and demise.

During Wang Mang's reign, public discontentment grew, with people opposing the new ruler and longing for the previous Han dynasty, which helped propel Liu Xiu (6 BC–AD 57, reigned 25–57), a distant relative of the Western Han, to establish a new Han dynasty in the year AD 25. As this Han was established with Luoyang as the capital, a city to the east of Chang'an, the capital of Western Han, it became known as the Eastern Han dynasty in later years. Wang Mang's reign marked the boundary between the two Han dynasties, each lasting approximately 200 years, during which they shared fundamental political ideals and systems.

The Rise of Scholar-Official Elites

Beyond the stories of officials and Confucian scholars, there was another group of individuals who shaped Eastern Han politics. They were the key influencers and would become the creators of the heroic era that would emerge about 200 years later.

1. Previous Nobility, Merchants, and Wandering Adventurers

The Han dynasty inherited the agricultural focus from the previous Qin dynasty. Even today, farmers continue to comprise the majority of China's population, and agriculture remains the economic foundation of the country. Qin's emphasis on agriculture was determined by its geographical conditions and historical background. During the Spring and Autumn and the Warring States periods, the construction of cities in feudal states provided opportunities for the development of urban commerce and industry. Compared to Qin, the other states in China had more developed commerce and industry, allowing merchants to travel between regions and adventurers through the alleys and streets of cities. Lü Buwei (d. 235 BC), who assisted Qin Shihuang in his unification efforts, was a prominent merchant doing business in the capital of Zhao, Handan. Youxia (or wandering adventurers) were a unique group, particularly during the Qin and Han periods. Not engaged in production and living a wandering life, they had low social status. Associating with elite society, many of them lived on the periphery of political life. Some were wealthy, some were not, some were chivalrous, and some were troublemakers. Liu Bang, the founder of the Western Han dynasty, could be considered an adventurer himself, to some extent.

Like Lü Buwei, the previous nobility, wealthy merchants, and wandering adventurers from the six other states contributed significantly to the founding of the Qin and Han dynasties. However, they were also the primary targets of suppression when the dynasties were securely established. For instance, Emperor Wu of Han utilized various measures such as relocating affluent local groups, monopolizing the salt and iron trades, and levying property taxes on merchants to counteract these influential economic groups, preventing them from threatening his rule. At the same time, he reduced forced labor, lowered taxes and provided honorary awards to support small-scale agricultural economies. The Qin and Han empires attempted to weaken these influential groups and redirect societal production towards agriculture and small-scale handicrafts based in rural areas, while encouraging individual small farmers to engage in simple material exchanges within the road and market networks established since pre-Qin times. This was aimed at sustaining the operation of the empire. Consequently, the empire's reach extended directly to the grassroots level without interference from intermediate powers.

However, the policy of restraining merchants encouraged people to cultivate more land but, at the same time, would hinder farmers from effectively utilizing the market. More importantly, as the population increased, land became increasingly scarce, and it became harder for farmers to sustain their livelihoods and engage in simple reproduction. Meanwhile, the influential tended to purchase and operate more land in rural areas. At the same time, due to the production conditions at the time, large estates could manage to meet the needs of simple reproduction and the livelihoods and production activities of the individual farmers through "closed-door market" practices. The government could no longer provide more land to farmers, and attempts such as those by Wang Mang to redistribute land among farmers according to ancient systems ended in failure. At this point, the government had to compromise with the emerging landlords of the large estates, who are known as the "elite (powerful and dominant) families" of the Eastern Han dynasty.

2. Scholar-Official Elite Families

Unlike the "commoner generals and ministers" in the early Western Han dynasty, most of the founders of the Eastern Han dynasty came from the "hereditary scholar-official class." On one hand, they were local magnates with vast estates and diverse businesses, living in clan-based communities that attracted a large rural population. Some of them even possessed private militias. On the other hand, against the backdrop of implementing exclusive Confucianism, "scholars" with various backgrounds since the Warring States period gradually converged under the umbrella of Confucianism, no longer appearing as individual "wandering scholars." Those scholars who settled in the countryside took advantage of their family and clan influence, gradually monopolizing the educational and academic fields. During the Eastern Han period, scholars entered government service through recommendation or imperial summons, making studying classics to enter government service, especially at the central government level, the best career path for the children of elite families. Those recommended or summoned became proteges of the recommenders or local officials. Central bureaucrats formed groups with their proteges and former officials, increasing their political power. In the later period of the Eastern Han dynasty, there emerged some aristocratic families who were both local magnates and Confucian scholars. With high positions in the court and their proteges and former officials at different levels, they became leaders among the literati. In the later period of the Eastern Han dynasty, scholars were selected solely based on "family background," so the children of aristocratic families were favored in talent selection. At the local level, the influence of aristocratic families was even more monopolistic.

It can be said, therefore, that the Eastern Han regime was established on the basis of the rule of powerful clans from the very beginning. The founders of the Eastern Han, including Liu Xiu and his officials, were mostly from prominent families in the Central Plains, possessing both the identity of "scholars" and "aristocratic origin," demonstrating Confucian traits as well as political and military capabilities. As a result, Confucian thought spread far and wide through the prominent clans rather than the Confucian scholars who lacked a power base. During the Eastern Han, a group of renowned scholars emerged, specializing in the study of Confucian classics. While Confucianism gained the status of state religion, it also tended towards being mystified. Meanwhile, the prominent clans, through Confucian education, ascended to the political center. As the local clan forces grew during the Eastern Han, they gradually controlled local politics, economies, and military power. Eventually, these clans, who did not resemble the aristocrats of the pre-Qin era in origin, created one of the most celebrated periods in Chinese history—the Three Kingdoms period (220–280). This era witnessed a group of capable individuals, both learned and skilled in martial arts, with privileged backgrounds and abilities, performing romantic and tragic heroics in the annals of history.

Encountering Other Peoples

In 202 BC, the Han dynasty was established on the foundation of the Qin, the first unified dynasty in China. Lasting for over 400 years, it was among the major empires in the world with a highly developed civilization. The predominant inhabitants of this empire later adopted the fixed terms "Han people" or "Han Chinese." The pronunciation of "China" in English is believed to derive from the sound of "Qin," possibly originating from the term used by various countries in the Western Regions to refer to the Qin dynasty.

Our focus on Chinese history before the Qin and Han dynasties was primarily centered on the Central Plains, the core area of the Han Chinese. From the perspective of state formation, the significance of the Qin as a dynasty lies in its unification of China, effectively organizing the culturally similar states, which coexisted in the Central Plains region for several centuries, into a unified nation. However, after the establishment of the Qin and Han empires, the attention to Chinese history had to extend beyond the confines of the Central Plains.

1. Xiongnu and the Western Regions

Ever since the imperial period in China, powerful foreign states began to emerge as threats to the Central Plains dynasties, becoming an extremely important driving force shaping the course of Chinese history for the next 2000 years, persisting until modern times. These powerful foreign entities typically originated from the northern grasslands and comprised formidable nomadic tribes and kingdoms. Among them, the first nomadic kingdom to step onto the historical stage was the Xiongnu, remaining a powerful adversary throughout the Qin and Han dynasties.

The Xiongnu were a northern ethnic group that emerged during the late Warring States period. Around the time of Qin's unification of the six states, they gradually conquered some tribes on the Mongolian Plateau, establishing a powerful grassland empire extending south to the Yin Mountains and north to Lake Baikal. They then expanded southward, occupying the Hetao region, i.e., the Yellow River floodplain south of the Yin Mountains, posing a significant threat to the Qin dynasty. This prompted Qin Shihuang to dispatch a 300,000-strong

army to attack the Xiongnu, relocate settlers to open up land for cultivation in northern frontiers, and build the Great Wall, a world-renowned feat of engineering. At the outset, the Han dynasty was not powerful enough to contend with the Xiongnu and had to resort to diplomatic measures such as that of marriage alliance to stabilize the northern border. However, during the strategic reign of Emperor Wu of Han, the dynasty gradually gained the upper hand against the Xiongnu. They not only regained control of the Hetao region in the Yellow River basin, lost since the time of Qin Shihuang, but also dealt significant blows to the Xiongnu forces, forcing them to migrate further north.

In the historical confrontation between the Han and the Xiongnu, it was not the Xiongnu's retreat that truly influenced the future of China; instead, it perhaps had a more significant impact on the Western historical process. For China, the significance lay in the connection between the Central Plains and the Western Regions. It was precisely through the interceptions against the Xiongnu that the Han gained control of the Hexi Corridor (located in the northwest part of present Gansu Province), a narrow corridor situated between the Central Plains, the Mongolian Plateau, and the Qinghai-Tibet Plateau. Beyond Dunhuang at the western end of the Hexi Corridor lies the ancient Western Regions, which correspond to present-day Xinjiang in northwestern China and Central Asia. In the early Western Han period, the Xiongnu extended their influence to the Western Regions. During the reign of Emperor Wu, the Yuezhi, who had previously inhabited the Hexi Corridor and later migrated westward after being attacked by the Xiongnu, harbored intentions of retaliating against the Xiongnu. Emperor Wu of Han sought to ally with them to attack the Xiongnu. Consequently, Zhang Qian (d. 114 BC) became the first envoy of the Western Han to open up

Fig. 29 Zhang Qian's Mission to the Western Regions
Tang dynasty (618–907)
North Wall of Cave 323, Mogao Grottoes, Dunhuang, Gansu Province

communication with the Western Regions. Zhang Qian embarked on two missions, enduring hardships over more than 20 years. Although he did not achieve substantive political objectives, his journeys to the Western Regions integrated the Xinjiang region with the Central Plains for the first time in history, signifying a momentous development (fig. 29).

During the Eastern Han period, the Xiongnu split into two factions, with the southern horde residing to the north of the Han and submitting to Han rule, while the northern horde initially retained control over the Western Regions and frequently invaded the northern borders and areas along the Hexi Corridor of the Han dynasty. However, under the Eastern Han's military campaigns, the Northern Xiongnu eventually migrated westward and assimilated into other ethnic groups. The vast region north of Gobi (i.e., the northern part of China's desert and the Gobi Desert) gradually came under the control of emerging nomadic tribes, notably

The Dunhuang Grottoes, combining grotto architecture, painted sculptures, and murals, are the most dazzling artistic treasure trove along the ancient Silk Road. The image is a representative work, composed of three scenes. The upper right depicts the emperor worshiping a Buddha statue, the lower right shows Zhang Qian bidding farewell to the emperor, and the upper left illustrates Zhang Qian arriving in the Western Regions, reflecting the Tang dynasty Buddhist followers' understanding and imagination of Zhang Qian's mission to the Western Regions.

the Xianbei. Similar to Zhang Qian of the Western Han, Ban Chao (32–102) served as an envoy to the Western Regions during the Eastern Han period. He hailed from a family of historians, and his elder brother was Ban Gu, the renowned compiler of the historical text *Book of Han*, mentioned earlier. Ban Chao's missions to the Western Regions were part of the Eastern Han court's strategy to militarily subdue the Northern Xiongnu, aiming to establish connections with the rulers of various Western Region states, detach them from the Xiongnu, and align them with the Eastern Han. Over his 30-year tenure of missions to the Western Regions, Ban Chao restored Eastern Han control over the Western Regions and the traffic between the Central Plains and the Western Regions, so as to facilitate continued economic and cultural exchanges between the two vast regions.

Fig. 30 Brocade Armguard
Han dynasty
Length 18.5 cm, width 12.5 cm
Xinjiang Museum

This Shu brocade armguard was unearthed at the Niya site in Hotan, Xinjiang. It bears the inscription "Five stars rise in the east, benefiting China," indicating that during the Han dynasty, people used astrology to pray for the prosperity of the country. Shu brocade could only be produced in Chang'an in present-day Shaanxi Province and Chengdu in present-day Sichuan Province, representing the highest level of silk weaving craftsmanship. The Niya site was a crucial location on the southern route of the Silk Road, highlighting the close connection between the Western Regions and the Central Plains during the Han period.

2. The Silk Road

During the Han dynasty, overland trade routes were opened between East Asia and the Western Regions, across the Hexi Corridor and Tianshan mountain ranges in Xinjiang Uygur Autonomous Region, gradually extending even further west. The two routes passing south of the Tianshan Mountains and the oasis countries on the southern and northern edges of the Tarim Basin became the major thoroughfares for economic and cultural exchanges between ancient China and the West. Because the earliest, largest, and most important commodity that spread along this trade route was Chinese silk (fig. 30), and since the emergence of Chinese silk has had a far-reaching impact on world history and civilization, these traffic routes through Chang'an, the Hexi Corridor, the Tianshan Corridor, to Central Asia and even further west are therefore known as the Silk Road.

In the early 1990s, the Xuanquanzhi Posthouse, a relay station along the Han dynasty Silk Road, where mails were

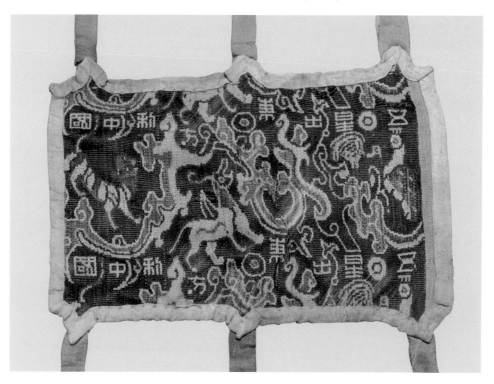

Fig. 31 Located in Dunhuang, Gansu Province, the Xuanquanzhi Posthouse on the vast Gobi Desert bears witness to the invaluable historical exchanges between the Han dynasty and various Western Regions states, embodying the prosperity of the Silk Road.

delivered or received and accommodations were provided for tradesmen, was discovered (fig. 31). About 60 kilometers east of present-day Dunhuang City in Gansu Province, it is the earliest and most well-preserved postal station to date. Over 30,000 Han bamboo slips were unearthed, containing not only imperial edicts, horse training manuals, and postal letters but also rental records of the horses and carriages and guestrooms in the station. Among thousands of clerks working for the station in several centuries before it was deserted, one named Hong was identified. Working years in the position, the grassroots official served monarchs from kingdoms in Western Regions and their envoys, commissioners appointed by the Han court to handle local affairs, and Han princesses engaged in diplomatic marriages with the royal families in remote kingdoms. The more than 70 slips in which Hong was mentioned relate a relay station and its minor official with a much larger world. This station, however, was among thousands of stations belonging to the Han empire.

This chapter has offered a fascinating glimpse of life in the Qin and Han dynasties.

The unearthed bamboo slips and documents allow us to see how the vast empire was ruled at the grassroots level, where ordinary people labored for a living. From the perspective of world history, we see how the grassroots commoners were involved in encounters with the "alien races." The Huaxia, who had already succeeded in molding a Chinese identity, had their first large-scale conflicts and exchanges with the nomadic tribes from the north. The order of Huaxia's world was re-established during the Qin and Han dynasties, as they, influenced by Confucianism, redefined their roles in various social strata. At the same time, they evaluated the heterogeneous worlds of the Western Regions and the northern tribes from the perspective of their own agrarian culture. This re-establishment of interpersonal relationships in the early imperial era laid a profound foundation for the subsequent development of Chinese history.

CHAPTER FOUR
Flowers In The Midst of Hell: Three Kingdoms, Two Jins, and Northern and Southern Dynasties

The Han dynasty, spanning approximately four hundred years, has long been revered in China as an exemplary period of imperial rule characterized by advanced civilization and enduring unity. However, with the collapse of the Han, imperial China entered its longest phase of fragmentation, lasting for another four hundred years and witnessing the rise and fall of over twenty influential regimes. This era was marred by warfare, massacres, and bloodshed, and not only ordinary citizens but also the ruling class suffered from uncertainty and unpredictability.

Despite the turmoil and chaos, amidst this bloody period, glimpses of humanity and artistic beauty persisted. Some nobles even sought an aesthetic sense of spiritual transcendence through acts of self-sacrifice. It was akin to dancing a splendid waltz in a dazzling ballroom, only to be abruptly thrust into the depths of hell, leaving behind a legacy of melancholy and contemplation for future generations. This era transformed the once tranquil and somewhat mundane human world into a hellish realm where individuals danced precariously on the edge of a blade.

On the facing page

Fig. 32 *Peach Blossom Spring* (detail). Please refer to pages 68–69 for more information of the painting.

The Many Heroes

Towards the end of the Eastern Han dynasty, political corruption soared, and civil unrest became widespread. Concurrently, folk witchcraft practices began to blend with Taoist teachings, giving rise to early Taoism. This form of Taoism incorporated elements of Yin-Yang theories and was influenced by the theistic aspects of Confucianism, embracing prophetic imagery.

In AD 184, Zhang Jue (?–184), the leader of the Way of Supreme Peace, a Taoist movement, spearheaded the Yellow Turban Rebellion, rallying his followers, known as the "Yellow Turban Army," against the Eastern Han court. Although the rebellion was swiftly quelled by influential local families across Eastern Han territories, it exposed the court's inability to maintain control over its local governments, hastening its decline.

This tumultuous period, known as the Three Kingdoms era, later became a prominent subject in historical narratives.

I. Three Kingdoms

The Three Kingdoms era marked a period of China's division into three distinct dynastic states: Wei (220–265), Shu Han (221–263), and Wu (221–280), following the fall of the Han dynasty. These three kingdoms were established respectively by Cao Cao (155–220) and his son Cao Pi (187–226), Liu Bei (161–223), and Sun Quan (182–252) during the late Eastern Han dynasty. The Ming dynasty (1368–1644) novel *Romance of the Three Kingdoms* has had a profound influence on Chinese culture, shaping public perception of this era as a time of heroic figures and epic struggles.

In the novel, the founder of the Wei state, Cao Cao, hails from a family of eunuchs and is renowned for his cunning and scheming nature. The founder of the Shu state, Liu Bei, is a descendant of the Han imperial family and dedicates his life to the revival of the Han dynasty. Though his loyalty is sometimes tinged with hypocrisy, he unquestionably stands as the protagonist of the novel. The founder of the Wu state, Sun Quan, is portrayed with a rather one-dimensional and subdued personality, often serving as a supporting character to drive the plot forward.

The most well-known figure in the novel is Zhuge Liang (181–234), the Prime Minister of Shu Han. Renowned for his wit and wisdom, he demonstrated remarkable foresight from a young age. Devoting himself to assisting the emperor until his death, Zhuge Liang became a symbol of loyalty and righteousness. He enjoyed high prestige in his territory, present-day Chengdu in Sichuan Province, where the Wuhou Shrine honors him (fig. 33). This shrine also houses a shrine for Liu Bei. The joint shrine for a ruler and his minister is exceedingly rare in China, reflecting their harmonious relationship.

Additionally, the novel depicts the famous deity in Han culture, the God of Wealth, Guan Gong, whose prototype was the renowned general of Shu, Guan Yu (?–220), as Liu Bei's sworn brother, another figure celebrated for his loyalty (fig. 34).

2. The North-South Standoff

The *Romance of the Three Kingdoms* is indeed more of a literary fiction than a strict historical account. Zhuge Liang, while portrayed in the novel with almost mythical

Fig. 33 The Wuhou Shrine Museum in Chengdu, Sichuan Province, which was built to honor Zhuge Liang; one of the most common portrayals in Chinese film and television productions.

Fig. 34 The Temple to commemorate Guan Gong in Jingzhou, Hubei Province. Through millennia of cultural evolution, Guan Yu, revered as the God of War due to the stories from the Three Kingdoms period (220–280), has transcended reality and become a spiritual symbol for many people.

qualities, was not truly god-like in historical reality, nor was Guan Yu gentleman-like. Cao Cao, on the other hand, possessed a charismatic personality, renowned for his exceptional military and political talents as well as his skill as a first-rate writer and poet. Likewise, Sun Quan was not devoid of worldly wisdom and could be considered a hero in his own right.

Cao Cao won battles against formidable opponents during the tumultuous late Eastern

Han dynasty, consolidating the unification of northern China. However, his southern expansion faced staunch resistance from Sun Quan, who commanded the lower Yangtze River basin, and Liu Bei, who controlled a portion of the middle Yangtze basin. This was the Battle of Chibi (northwest of present-day Chibi City, Hubei Province), a famous battle in history in which the few defeated the many. Subsequently, Liu Bei capitalized on the situation by seizing control of the Sichuan region in the upper Yangtze River basin, while Sun Quan expanded his influence into the middle Yangtze basin. Thus, the framework of the Three Kingdoms was established.

These three regimes were all established on the premise of effectively managing local powerful clans and aristocratic families. However, the strength of these clans varied, leading to different trajectories in the founding of the Three Kingdoms. For example, the clans in Shu were the weakest, so Liu Bei's establishment of his kingdom was relatively swift; he declared himself emperor and founded his country seven years after seizing control of Shu. The clans in Wu were relatively strong, so Sun Quan's path to founding his kingdom seemed to be longer; he established his rule earlier but declared himself emperor the latest. Wei had the most formidable strength, occupying the Central Plains region, the traditional political center of China. As direct successors of the Han dynasty, Wei possessed the most legitimacy in ruling and adopted measures to win over powerful clans, among which the most famous measure was implementing a system of electing officials that guaranteed the hereditary privilege of prominent clans in official positions. Because Wei was the strongest among the Three Kingdoms, Shu and Wu formed a long-term alliance to counter the northern threat.

The emergence of the Three Kingdoms marked an unprecedented change in the Chinese geopolitical landscape, representing the first instance of a standoff between the southern and northern regions. Behind this division was the economic and population growth in the south during the Han dynasty, which provided the resources necessary for its prolonged confrontation with the north.

A Chaotic Era

Amidst the valor of their numerous heroes, the three states engaged in decades of military confrontations spanning two or three generations, yet none emerged as the ultimate victor. The Sima family, descendants of Sima Yi (179–251) who once served Cao Cao, seized control of Wei and, in AD 263, annihilated the state of Shu. Subsequently, Sima Yan (236–290), the grandson of Sima Yi, established the Jin dynasty (265–420) to replace Wei. This new dynasty, commonly referred to as the Western Jin (265–316), eradicated the Wu regime in AD 280, once again achieving national unity. However, this unified China lasted a little more than two decades before descending into a more intense and prolonged period of division.

I. The Rise and Fall of Western Jin

For a newly unified dynasty, achieving stability in governance typically requires around thirty years of concerted effort. Founding monarchs often possess a heightened awareness of public sentiment, implementing policies aimed at alleviating social tensions. However, the ruling elite of the Western Jin dynasty swiftly succumbed to excessive decadence and opulence. For instance, Emperor Sima Yan's harem boasted nearly ten thousand female servants, an astounding figure. This extravagance permeated the nobility, with some burning candles as firewood and others laying silk carpets spanning twelve miles along the main roads leading to their residences. The widespread practice of buying and selling official positions further exacerbated matters.

This state of affairs stemmed primarily from Sima Yan's noble lineage, which left him disconnected from common life experiences. Moreover, during the establishment of the Sima family's rule over Wei, societal upheavals caused by war had not occurred, rendering it challenging to alter existing social structures. Since the decline of the Eastern Han dynasty, powerful clans had risen, giving rise to successive generations of families holding influential positions within the government, thereby forming prominent aristocratic families. In a way, the Sima family's ascension to power occurred with the support of these influential aristocratic families. Consequently, politically and economically favorable policies had to be implemented to appease these influential factions.

After usurping the throne as a powerful minister, Sima Yan, once in power, took precautions against his own influential ministers. He attributed Wei's decline to the lack of support from the imperial clans. Consequently, he bestowed princely titles upon his family members, granting them significant administrative and military authority, hoping they would fulfill the role of upholding the imperial family. This reform could be effective when the emperor possessed adeptness in governing and could exercise power freely. However, after Sima Yan's death in 290, his successor proved incapable of controlling the political landscape, leading to intense power struggles within the ruling clique. The following year, serious armed conflicts erupted among eight royal princes, resulting in what history remembers as the "War of the Eight Princes."

2. Nomadic Tribes Moving Inward

As the global climate cooled from the 3rd to the 6th century AD, nomadic tribes from the north were compelled to migrate to warmer southern regions. Crossing the traditional agricultural-pastoral border demarcated by the Great Wall, this resulted in a cohabitation scenario between Han Chinese and non-Han ethnic groups in northern China. Among the sizable non-Han population in North China during the Western Jin dynasty, the Xiongnu stood out prominently. Spanning the extensive territories of present-day Shanxi and Shaanxi provinces, they were descendants of the Southern Xiongnu who had submitted to the Han dynasty during the Eastern Han period. Suggestions had been made to relocate these ethnic minorities, aiming to separate them from the Han populace due to perceived governmental threats, yet these proposals were unsuccessful. During the latter stages of the War of the Eight Princes, these ethnic groups became embroiled in the conflicts, some coerced and others volunteering, in pursuit of potential advantages. Eventually, they emerged victorious. In AD 316, the Xiongnu brought an end to the Western Jin dynasty and established their own regime in northern China, marking the first time a nomadic tribe had established rule in the Central Plains region traditionally inhabited by the Han Chinese.

From AD 190 to 316, China experienced two periods of division during the Eastern Han and Western Jin dynasties, each driven by distinct issues. The Eastern Han fractured due to conflicts between central authority and powerful local clans, and the court was unable to control the rising local power, with the Yellow Turban Rebellion serving as a trigger. Conversely, the decline of the Western Jin was primarily attributed to ethnic tensions, as nomadic tribes continuously migrated southward, challenging the established social and political order. These developments marked the emergence of local clan dynamics and ethnic conflicts as significant factors shaping China's unity and division.

3. Succession of Regimes amidst Turmoil

Following the collapse of the Western Jin, with the migration of groups such as the Xiongnu and Xianbei to the north of the Great Wall, the Gaoche people became the new rulers of the Mongolian Plateau. This marked the period of the "Sixteen Kingdoms" (304–439) in northern China, primarily established by five non-Han ethnic groups: the Xiongnu, Xianbei, Jie, Di, and Qiang, forming sixteen (actually nineteen) regimes. In opposition to them, the Eastern Jin stood in the south, followed by the Song dynasty (Liu-Song) of the Southern dynasties (420–589).

At the collapse of the Western Jin, Sima Rui (276–323), a member of the Sima family originally associated with the Wei dynasty, crossed the Yangtze River. With support from powerful clans like the Wang Dao and others from the north, he seized the throne and established the Eastern Jin regime. Due to the weakened imperial power, over the century-long history of the Eastern Jin, there arose instances where families such as the Wang Dao, Yu Liang, Xie An, and Huan Wen, alongside the imperial Sima family, collectively wielded authority—a unique phenomenon in Chinese history resulting from the culmination of aristocratic politics since the late Eastern Han period. This endured for over a century due to the internal power structure's equilibrium, particularly the balance between the imperial family and the influential clans, as well as among these clans. However, with time, these influential clans gradually became more and more corrupt and waned in political potency, challenging the maintenance of this equilibrium. Consequently, this political landscape eventually came to an end as the Eastern Jin was supplanted by the Liu-Song dynasty (known as the Song of the Southern dynasties).

Mingshi

From the onset of the Yellow Turban Rebellion, the era spanning the Three Kingdoms and Jin Dynasties (or Two Jins) was marked by a tumultuous blend of military conflicts, epidemics, and political unrest, affecting both the common people and the elite, who found themselves navigating constant uncertainty. As a result, established traditions, personal ideologies, scholarly knowledge, and religious beliefs were all called into question. For many influential clans, the philosophy of "eat, drink, and be merry" became prevalent, dismissing the practicality and even the sincerity of traditional classics. A social entity, known as mingshi, or "celebrated scholars," evolved into an archetype embodying this mindset.

1. Seven Sages of the Bamboo Grove

During the Three Kingdoms and Two Jins periods, the "Seven Sages of the Bamboo Grove" represented a group of scholars, artists, and musicians from noble families: Ruan Ji, Ji Kang, Shan Tao, Xiang Xiu, Liu Ling, Wang Rong, and Ruan Xian (see fig. 35 on pages 64–65). They frequently gathered in a bamboo grove in Shanyang County, possibly in the vicinity of present-day Yuntai Mountain in Xiuwu County, Henan Province. There, they enjoyed a simple, rustic lifestyle centered around wine and the arts, earning them the title of "Seven Sages." In *Shishuo Xinyu* (also known as *A New Account of Tales of the World*), a chronicle of notable individuals from the late Eastern Han to the Three Kingdoms and Two Jins periods, Ji Kang (223–262) is described in exaggerated terms, likening his presence to a towering solitary pine tree, standing proudly alone. When intoxicated, he was said to resemble a massive jade mountain on the brink of toppling. This exaggerated depiction aimed to capture his exceptional

inner character with a graceful visual image, reflecting the aesthetic ideals and pursuits of the upper-class scholars during the Three Kingdoms, Two Jins, and Northern and Southern dynasties (420–589). However, despite Ji Kang's remarkable demeanor and his marital ties to the Wei dynasty's royal family, he was eventually sent to the execution ground by Sima Zhao (211–265), the man who put an end to Cao Wei's regime, on the charge of violating traditional moral principles. Even before his execution, Ji Kang reportedly remained composed and requested to play the ancient zither. Thus, this intellectual, musician, and writer of the Wei period met his demise at the age of forty.

So, what kind of behavior could be deemed as violating traditional moral principles? Let's take the case of Ruan Ji (210–263), a renowned poet and close companion of Ji Kang, for instance. During the mourning period for his mother, he attended a banquet hosted by Sima Zhao, where he drank and ate meat with a calm demeanor. Such conduct ran counter to the moral values upheld by the Sima family, which emphasized governing the country with filial piety, and would have been looked down upon by adherents of traditional etiquette. However, were the actions of these intellectuals, such as drinking, reveling, and indulging, truly arrogant and decadent? Quite the opposite. Amidst

the frequent changes of dynasties and the turmoil of politics, the upper echelons of society witnessed exceptionally brutal power struggles. The prominent families were often swept into the whirlwind of political turmoil, living in a precarious situation despite their wealth and comfort. It is said that Ruan Ji leaned politically towards the imperial family of the Wei dynasty and harbored discontent

towards the Sima family faction. However, he also realized the futility of meddling in worldly affairs, so he adopted a stance of non-involvement and prudent self-preservation. In an attempt to win Ruan Ji over, Sima Zhao proposed a marriage alliance, but Ruan Ji, in order to evade the proposal, indulged in heavy drinking every day, getting intoxicated for sixty consecutive days. Eventually, Sima

Fig. 35 Brick Painting of the Seven Sages of the Bamboo Grove and Rong Qiqi
Southern dynasties (420–589)
Nanjing Museum, Jiangsu Province

The brick painting consists of over 200 ancient tomb bricks. It depicts the Seven Sages of the Bamboo Grove and Rong Qiqi, another historical figure of the same period. Each figure is separated by ginkgo, locust tree, pine, and willow trees. The figures are seated on the ground in various poses, fully expressing the free and idealistic personalities of the scholar-gentry intellectuals. Closer details of Ji Kang (left) and Ruan Ji (right) could be found in the lower-middle of this spread.

Zhao, feeling powerless, remarked, "Ah, forget it; let this drunkard be!" Ruan Ji managed to preserve his life for the time being, leading him to lament in his poetry: "I've been treading on thin ice all my life; who knows how troubled I am!"

As elite members of noble families, many individuals were destined for high positions from the very beginning of their lives. They were also aware that they would be swept into ruthless political whirlpools. Since this was a collective fate for them, some of them chose to live fully in the present moment. They drank, practiced alchemy in pursuit of immortality, traveled through mountains and rivers, and composed poetry and essays. Ultimately, it was their reflection on what it means to be human. It is precisely because of the awakening of "human" consciousness that during the Three Kingdoms and Two Jins periods, China witnessed the first peak in literature and art in its history.

2. Wang Xizhi and Xie An

Wang Xizhi (303–361), the most celebrated and influential calligrapher in China, was born into an aristocratic family in Langya, Shandong Province, during the Eastern Jin dynasty. He rose to fame at a young age and began his career in government service in his youth. However, in his middle age, he surprised many by solemnly vowing at his parents' gravesite never to serve in government again, causing a significant stir in the Eastern Jin court. After resigning from his official position, Wang Xizhi relocated to the Shanyin County of Kuaiji Prefecture (present-day Shaoxing City, Zhejiang Province in East China), where he constructed a library, planted mulberry trees, taught students, composed poetry and essays, and practiced painting and calligraphy (fig. 36). He found joy in fishing and raising geese.

Xie An (320–385), who once learned calligraphy from Wang Xizhi, hailed from another top aristocratic family of the Eastern Jin dynasty, the Xie clan. Gifted in various fields from a young age, including calligraphy, music, and philosophy, he refused to take up official positions, choosing instead to live in seclusion on Mount Dongshan in Shaoxing, where he enjoyed the company of intellectuals and the pleasures of nature. It was only after the passing of many influential figures from his clan in the court that he returned to prominence.

In 383, Fu Jian, the ruler of the Former Qin dynasty (one of the Sixteen Kingdoms established by non-Han tribes), led a massive army southward, aiming to conquer the Eastern Jin dynasty and unify China. Despite the dire military situation and widespread fear in the capital of the Eastern Jin, Xie An

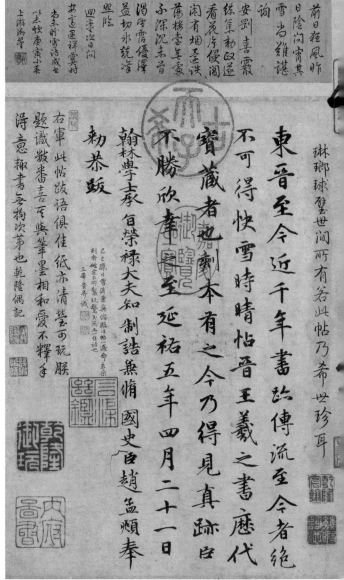

remained calm and composed. He dispatched his younger relatives to lead troops to resist the invasion. By the end of the year, the two sides clashed at Feishui (southeast of present-day Shouxian County, Anhui Province in East China). The Battle of Feishui is a remarkable parallel to the Battle of Chibi during the Three Kingdoms period, the outnumbered Eastern Jin forces achieved a resounding victory over the Former Qin army. This victory solidified the rule of the Eastern Jin dynasty while causing the

Fig. 36 Tang Dynasty Replica of *Timely Clearing After Snowfall*
Wang Xizhi (303–361)
Ink on paper
Length 14.8 cm, height 23 cm
Palace Museum, Taibei

This calligraphy piece conveys greetings to friends after heavy snowfall. It profoundly influenced the aesthetic appreciation of Chinese calligraphy and was treasured by emperors in later generations.

have already defeated the enemy." It was only after finishing the game and bidding farewell to his guest that Xie An could no longer contain his joy. He danced around the room, breaking the teeth of the wooden clogs he wore. The victory at the Battle of Feishui elevated Xie An's reputation to its peak. However, he voluntarily relinquished his power to avoid trouble.

Xie An was later acclaimed as the "Elegant Prime Minister," and the word "elegance" precisely encapsulated the lives of scholars during the Two Jins periods. Because of such individuals, therefore, the era, despite being a time of chaos, is referred by some historians as China's true "aristocratic age." These scholars often hailed from prestigious families, received a fine education in literature and the arts, were renowned literary figures or artists, and inevitably either influenced or were influenced by the political landscape. However, despite the admiration for these intellectuals at the time, when a frivolous and libertine lifestyle or personal pleasures became societal norms, even transforming into a pursuit of sensory thrills and physical indulgence, the negative effects of such trends gradually became apparent. With the unification of the northern territories by the Xianbei-led Northern Wei dynasty (386–557), the dynamic of previously weak North and strong South began to reverse. The wheels of history ultimately shattered the delicate demeanor of the literati, propelling society in a more robust and vigorous direction.

temporary unity in the north to crumble, marking another significant turning point in Chinese history.

Legend has it that when news of the Jin army's triumph over the Former Qin reached Xie An, he was playing chess with a guest. After reading the victory report, he casually placed it beside him and continued playing chess without any change in expression. When his guest could no longer contain their curiosity and asked about his reaction, Xie An calmly replied, "It's nothing. The kids

Peach Blossom Spring

Tao Yuanming (c. 365–427), regarded by later generations as a representative recluse scholar of the Eastern Jin dynasty, once wrote a story about a fisherman from Wuling Prefecture (present-day Changde City, Hunan Province). While fishing, he chanced upon a forest of blossoming peach trees. Beyond the dense woods was an idyllic village with picturesque surroundings. The villagers lived a happy, free, and equal life, without the need for government oversight. They claimed that their ancestors had fled the chaos of the Qin dynasty to settle there, completely isolated from the outside world for hundreds of years, unaware of subsequent events and the history of the Three Kingdoms and Two Jins periods. They cautioned the fisherman not to reveal the location to others. However, the fisherman did not keep his promise and, upon leaving, brought local officials to search for the Peach Blossom Spring, but was never again able to find an entrance. This story is widely circulated in China and has given rise to the idiom "Shiwai Taoyuan" (literally the Land of Peach Blossoms), meaning "utopia." (fig. 37)

Fig. 37 *Peach Blossom Spring* (detail)
Qiu Ying (c. 1501–c. 1551)
Ink and color on paper
Length 472 cm, height 33 cm
Museum of Fine Arts, Boston

The artist uses azure blue and malachite green to create the land of Peach Blossom Spring, depicting it as an ethereal paradise where the realms of immortals and humans intertwine. The scene is magnificent and tranquil.

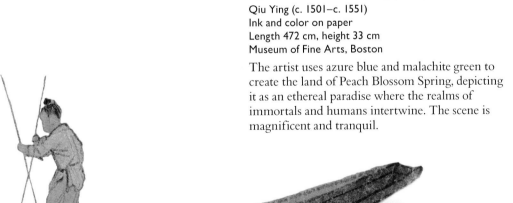

I. Two Countermeasures

The tale of Peach Blossom Spring is often viewed as an idyllic creation of Tao Yuanming's imagination, yet to a certain extent, it mirrors the social realities of its time. Throughout the periods of the Three Kingdoms, Two Jins, and the Northern and Southern dynasties, the heartland of China was engulfed in relentless turmoil. Amidst the turmoil and widespread violence, ordinary people lived in constant fear for their lives. Some prominent clans led their followers in migrating southward with the Jin dynasty, while others relocated their entire clans to the mountains, establishing fortified villages known as "wubi." Originating from the Han dynasty, wubi were small fortresses built for defensive purposes, typically situated on flat terrain with surrounding walls, front and back gates, an internal watchtower, corner towers, resembling the layout of a city. Many opted to migrate under the protection of local prominent clans for survival. Following the collapse of the Western Jin dynasty, wubi became a common sight across the Central Plains. The leaders of these wubi were predominantly elite Han Chinese who fortified their defenses through these structures and organized private militias. Within the confines of the wubi, a self-sustaining agrarian economy thrived, centered around production and consumption. Towards the twilight of the Han dynasty, certain influential wubi leaders implemented policies of collective production and consumption within their fortified settlements (fig. 38).

If the wubi were constructed by powerful clans for military and economic purposes during the turbulent era, it also served as a haven for common people. Religion, on the other hand, was another antidote to the chaotic world. Unlike the predominance of Confucianism in the intellectual sphere during the Han dynasties, there was a significant ideological shift during this period. Among the literati, there was a trend of "metaphysics (xuanxue)", characterized by interpreting Confucian classics through the lens of Taoist philosophers like Laozi and Zhuangzi. This study aimed to elucidate the

Fig. 38 During the Wei (220–265) and Jin periods in the Hexi region, brick murals often depict the wubi. Though roughly drawn, these murals reveal thick surrounding walls with defensive battlements atop them, and within the courtyard stand tall towers for observation and shooting.

Fig. 39 *Whiling Away the Summer* (detail)
Liu Guandao (Yuan dynasty, 1271–1368)
Ink and color on silk
Length 71.2 cm, height 29.3 cm
Nelson-Atkins Museum of Art

This figure painting depicts a scholar reclining on a couch, holding a deer's tail whisk in his right hand and a book in his left hand, forming a tranquil and elegant scene.

concepts of the "Tao" and "Nothingness," representing the eternal and unchanging spiritual essence beyond the tangible world, ineffable in words. It became fashionable for intellectuals to engage in elegant discussions of this philosophy while holding a refined utensil made from the tail hair of deer or similar animals, known as "Buddhist Dust." This highly abstract metaphysical thought differed from Confucianism as it did not delve into state affairs or worldly matters. While it briefly gained popularity in intellectual circles, it primarily served as a status symbol for the aristocracy to display their refinement, rather than deeply influencing various social strata (fig. 39).

Metaphysics emerged as a fusion of Confucianism and Taoist ideas, but the Taoist School and later Taoism reached its zenith during the Three Kingdoms, Two Jins, and Northern and Southern dynasties. It assimilated local indigenous religions, shamanistic practices, and diverse methods related to deities and immortality, evolving into a regional religion with numerous sects, intricate rituals, and a diverse array of adherents.

2. Flourishing Buddhism

Buddhism, introduced from India during the Han dynasty, saw its initial flourishing in China during the Two Jins periods. Buddhist scriptures were widely translated, and a cohort of esteemed translators emerged. Chinese monks embarked on journeys to India in pursuit of Buddhist teachings. The translators of Buddhist scriptures borrowed concepts and terms from prevalent Taoist classics to interpret Buddhist scriptures, establishing theoretical links with metaphysics to facilitate their swift acceptance and popularity among the elite and bridging the gap between metaphysics and everyday life.

With the translation of more Buddhist scriptures into Chinese, the period following

the Eastern Jin dynasty
saw a proliferation of sects
interpreting Buddhist
teachings, often engaging
in intense debates.
Meanwhile, amidst
prolonged warfare, folk
beliefs in Buddhism were
becoming increasingly
widespread and deeply
entrenched. Despite
the division between
China along the Yangtze
River, there was frequent
exchange within the
Buddhist community
in the country. The
emperors of the Northern
Wei dynasty were
predominantly Buddhists,
and Emperor Wu of
Liang, Xiao Yan (reigned
502–549), was so devoted
to Buddhism that he
became a monk, earning
him the title of the
"Bodhisattva Emperor."

In one of his poems,
the Tang dynasty poet
Du Mu (803–853)
evokes the melancholy
and beauty of southern China, where "four
hundred and eighty temples stood in the
Southern dynasties, amidst mist and rain."
This is only a figment of the later generation,
and regrettably, none of the wooden temples
from the Southern dynasties have survived to
this day. However, many Buddhist grottoes
excavated in northern China during the same
period still stand as they did hundreds of years
ago. Among them are now world-famous
Yungang (fig. 40), Longmen, Dunhuang,
and Maijishan, most of which were initiated
during the Northern Wei dynasty. The
construction of temples and grottoes also
spurred the development of Buddhist murals

and paintings. Together, these surviving sites
showcase how Buddhism flourished in China
during its prime.

As a consequence, the Han dynasty's sole
veneration of Confucianism transitioned by
the time of the Three Kingdoms, Two Jins,
and Northern and Southern dynasties into
the coexistence and fusion of Confucianism,
Buddhism, and Taoism. Similarly, the
diverse expressions in poetry, painting,
and calligraphy experienced unparalleled
popularity and prosperity. Cultural and
artistic innovation endured amidst the
turbulent era, akin to flowers blooming in the
midst of hell.

Fig. 40 Initiated during the Northern Wei dynasty, the Yungang Grottoes in Datong, Shanxi Province, are one of China's three major grotto complexes, alongside the Longmen Grottoes in Luoyang, Henan Province, and the Mogao Grottoes in Dunhuang, Gansu Province. As the first grottoes authorized by imperial decree in China, the Yungang Grottoes reflect the political ambitions of the Northern Wei dynasty. They feature a mix of styles from other civilizations such as Indian and Central and West Asian artistic elements, highlighting their connections with major civilizations worldwide. This uniqueness in the treasury of Chinese art holds significant importance for the development of Chinese cultural and artistic heritage in later periods.

New Identity as "Chinese"

After the Sixteen Kingdoms period, the Northern Wei, established by the Tuoba Xianbei nomadic tribes, largely unified the north of China by the first half of the 5th century, confronting the dynasties of Song, Qi, and Liang in the south. China's history entered the era of the Northern and Southern dynasties. Meanwhile, the occupants north of the Great Wall shifted from the Gaoche to the Rouran, a confederacy of nomadic tribes.

Throughout the entirety of the Three Kingdoms, Two Jins, and Northern and Southern dynasties, the significance of

Northern Wei cannot be overstated. This dynasty achieved the longest-lasting unification of the northern regions, fundamentally reshaping the social fabric and historical course of Northern China. Governed by the Xianbei people, Northern Wei faced a cultural clash in administering the predominantly Han Chinese cultural territory of North China. The dilemma of whether to maintain their native culture for governance or to adopt Han Chinese culture confronted Tuoba Hong, Emperor Xiaowen (reigned 471–499) when he ascended the throne.

Throughout his nearly thirty-year reign, the first two decades were marked by the regency of his grandmother, Empress Dowager Feng, while the latter decade witnessed his personal reign. In both phases,

Chinese customs were favored for governance, but Emperor Xiaowen's approach was so radical that it amounted to an abandonment of his own cultural heritage. He endeavored to situate Northern Wei within the lineage of unified Chinese regimes, eschewing the inheritance of a nomadic regime like the Xiongnu Khanate or the Hu regimes of the Sixteen Kingdoms.

One of Emperor Xiaowen's decisive moves in the Sinicization reform was the relocation of the capital from Pingcheng (present-day Datong, Shanxi Province) to Luoyang, Henan Province. He cited Pingcheng's remoteness, emphasizing its association with military maneuver, while highlighting Luoyang's strategic location, suitable for unification and establishing imperial power. While his reasoning is valid, more importantly, as Luoyang was the former capital of the Western Jin dynasty, he sought to assert his legitimacy as the successor to the Jin dynasty. His decision demonstrated his ambition to break away from his own cultural traditions, further embracing Han Chinese heritage.

In Luoyang, Emperor Xiaowen implemented further reform measures. He mandated the conversion of Xianbei surnames to Chinese surnames. His own family name, Tuoba, was changed to the Chinese surname of Yuan, hence he was also known as Yuan Hong. Additionally, he prohibited the Xianbei people from wearing their traditional clothes, speaking their own language, and being buried in Pingcheng after death. These reforms were quite thorough, reflecting the emperor's admiration for Han culture and also highlighting the lack of a clear sense of ethnic cultural identity among the Xianbei community at that time. However, his reforms faced resistance within the ruling class.

The opposition primarily arose from those guarding the northern border, known as the "Six Garrisons Group." They were named as such because they constituted six military garrisons established by the Northern Wei to repel the Rouran invasion, situated north of the capital Pingcheng and south of the Yin Mountains. Among these six military districts, the most prominent was Wuchuan Garrison, which later gave rise to monarchs of the Northern Zhou, Sui (581–618), and Tang dynasties. Initially, these garrisons held significant political sway within the Northern Wei structure. However, following the capital's relocation to Luoyang and the process of Sinicization, a growing rift

Fig. 41 Song Dynasty Replica of *Northern Qi Scholars Collating Classic Texts*

Attributed to Yan Liben (c. 601–673)
Ink and color on silk
Length 144 cm, height 27.6 cm
Museum of Fine Arts, Boston

In the center of this scroll is a group of literati sitting on a couch, some deep in thought, others writing. It reflects the situation during the Northern Qi period, when there was a focus on compiling ancient texts and cultural integration among northern ethnic groups.

developed between the border guardians and the court. Eventually, the combination of demanding border defense duties, subpar living conditions, and dim political prospects exacerbated the conflicts. In AD 524, the generals of the six garrisons rebelled, eventually breaching the walls of Luoyang. The Northern Wei regime collapsed, lingering in a state of nominal existence. This historical event is known as the "Rebellion of the Six Garrisons."

During the later period of the Northern and Southern dynasties, Northern Wei underwent a division, giving rise to the Eastern Wei and Western Wei in opposition. However, power remained concentrated within two families: Gao Huan and Yuwen Tai, who soon supplanted the Wei regime and established Northern Qi and Northern Zhou respectively, perpetuating the conflict. They adhered to the traditional customs of Xianbei culture and upon assuming authority, enacted policies to reverse the previous Sinicization process.

During the Eastern Wei and Northern Qi periods, communication between the emperor and the nobility occurred in the Xianbei language, and instances of discrimination against the Han Chinese were prevalent. In the subsequent Western Wei and Northern Zhou periods, Han surnames were reverted back to Xianbei names. However, the aim of these reforms was not to revert to Xianbei traditions but to bridge the gap between the Six Garrisons and those relocated to Luoyang, thereby continuing the Sinicization process.

After numerous twists and turns, the distinctions between the two ethnicities gradually blurred, and conflicts between them diminished. The Xianbei evolved into "new Han Chinese," albeit with a penchant for equestrianism and a reverence for military achievements rather than solely lineage. Overall, the reforms of the Northern Zhou were more successful, which was one of the reasons that it was able to prevail over the more culturally advanced Northern Qi later (fig. 41 and refer to fig. 42 on pages 76–77 for details).

Meanwhile, to the north of the Great Wall, the Turkic Khanate, previously producing ironware for the Rouran Khanate, rebelled against them, swiftly achieving a decisive victory. The Turks emerged as an unprecedentedly powerful nomadic empire in history, ultimately gaining dominance over the Mongolian Plateau and Central Asia. Both the Rouran and the Turkic Khanate profoundly influenced the politics of Northern Qi and Northern Zhou, with the Turks assuming a dominant position. Northern Qi and Northern Zhou competed for friendship with, and even acknowledged vassalage to, the Turks. The central authorities in the Central Regions remained

Fig. 42 Closer details of Song Dynasty Replica of *Northern Qi Scholars Collating Classic Texts*.

in a weakened position until the advent of the later Sui dynasty.

During the same period, the Southern dynasties saw the successive reigns of the Song, Qi, Liang, and Chen dynasties. While the influence of aristocratic families waned and royal courts regained authority, the Southern dynasties were notably weakened.

By the time of the last dynasty, the Chen dynasty (557–589), the country's territory had contracted to nearly the size of Wu during the Three Kingdoms period. This suggests that the Northern dynasties (439–581) had secured a decisive advantage over the Southern dynasties, and reunification was inevitable.

CHAPTER FIVE
A New Age:
Sui and Tang Dynasties

The Sui and Tang dynasties are commonly considered the second most significant unified empire in Chinese history, following the Qin-Han period, which heralded China's entry into the imperial era. This era has a special significance both in world history and in Chinese history. Globally, this era witnessed China emerging as a major power in East Asia, with significantly increased interactions with the rest of the world. The Silk Road flourished, leading to extensive cultural exchanges that profoundly influenced China (fig. 44). From a Chinese historical perspective, it was a period of profound social transformation, marked by a shift from an aristocratic to a more egalitarian society.

◀ **Fig. 43** Closer details of Mural of Cave 220 at the Mogao Grottoes. Please refer to pages 90–91 and 94–95 for more information.

▼ **Fig. 44 Golden Bowl with Mandarin Duck and Lotus Petal Patterns**

Tang dynasty
Height 5.5 cm, diameter at mouth 13.7 cm
Shaanxi History Museum

The pure gold bowl was unearthed from the Hejiacun Kiln Site in Xi'an, Shaanxi Province. Hammered masterfully into shape, this bowl features two layers of outwardly convex lotus petals, with each lotus containing ten petals. Each lotus petal is intricately carved with animal and floral decorations. During the Tang dynasty, the Silk Road witnessed extensive exchanges between the East and the West, with a large quantity of exquisite Western gold and silverware imported into the Central Plains. This gold bowl demonstrates the adaptation and transformation of Western gold and silverware styles.

The Sui and Tang dynasties are often portrayed as powerful and open, exerting profound influence on the world around them. In many other countries, "Tang" became synonymous with China, and even today, areas where Chinese communities reside outside China are referred to as "Tangren Jie" (Chinatown) in Chinese. However, this focus on "cosmopolitanism" oversimplifies the era, neglecting the revolutionary changes that took place during this period. A pivotal moment occurred with the rebellion led by An Lushan and Shi Siming in AD 755. Following the rebellion, the Tang dynasty entered a period of about 150 years marked by distinct characteristics that sharply contrasted with the preceding era, which covers the same span of time.

Heading Towards Prosperity

The fragmentation of China, which endured for 400 years following the collapse of the Eastern Han dynasty, was ultimately brought to an end by the Northern Zhou and Sui dynasties. The Northern Zhou conquered the Northern Qi, consolidating control over the north. In AD 581, Yang Jian, the father-in-law of the Northern Zhou emperor, seized power and founded the Sui dynasty, thus formally inaugurating the era of the Sui-Tang empire.

1. Prelude for Cosmopolitanism

An exceptionally outstanding monarch, Yang Jian (541–604) not only conquered the last Southern dynasty, Chen, seven years after establishing the Sui dynasty, thereby achieving the reunification of the north and south, but he also implemented numerous significant political reforms during his reign. He ordered the construction of the city of Daxing to the southeast of the original Chang'an city, which later became the renowned international metropolis of

Tang Chang'an (today's Xi'an in Shaanxi Province in northwestern China). Among his many institutional innovations was an administrative model emphasizing the division of powers and checks and balances in the court. He also strengthened control over local authorities and the populace. His measures improved government efficiency and national capabilities, making the Sui dynasty an advanced state with a highly developed system of governance. Neighboring countries such as Japan and Silla (57 BC–AD 935) sent students to China to learn, signifying the beginning of the Sui-Tang as an empire of "cosmopolitanism."

After Yang Jian's death, his second son, Yang Guang, ascended to the throne as Emperor Yang of Sui (reigned 604–618). Possessing a character markedly different from his father's, Yang Guang was a monarch of considerable talent, imagination, and ambition. During his much shorter reign, he embarked on ambitious projects such as the construction of Luoyang city and the Grand Canal (fig. 45). In particular, the Grand Canal, with Luoyang as the center, linking Yuhang (present-day Hangzhou in southeastern China) and Zhuojun (present-day Beijing), significantly enhanced communication between the north and south, reshaping China's political, economic, and cultural landscape in the ensuing years. However, his emphasis on military expansion and exploitation of the populace heightened social tensions, ultimately leading to his demise and the collapse of the dynasty. Consequently, the Sui dynasty became synonymous with tyranny and brief rule.

The Sui dynasty, despite its short span of less than forty years, held a significant position in China's historical evolution akin to the Qin, the first imperial dynasty in China. The political groundwork established during the Sui period was crucial in facilitating the rapid national unification, social progress, and economic growth achieved during

Fig. 45 After Emperor Yang of Sui ascended the throne, he initiated large-scale renovations of the Grand Canal, connecting the north and south for the first time. The image shows the section of Yongji Canal (now known as Wei River) in Daokou Town, Anyang, Henan Province. The Yongji Canal was an important canal north of the Yellow River excavated in the Sui dynasty (581–618).

the subsequent Tang dynasty. Whether in familial ties or the fundamental principles of governance, the Tang dynasty represented more of a continuation of the Sui rather than a complete overthrow or rejection of it.

2. Emperor and Khan

The founder of the Tang dynasty, Li Yuan (566–635), had intricate connections with the royal families of both the Sui and Northern Zhou dynasties. They all originated from Wuchuan within the Six Garrisons of the Northern Wei and established themselves in the Guanlong region (present-day central Shaanxi Province and eastern Gansu Province

of China), together known historically as the "Guanlong Military Aristocracy Group." There were extensive marital relationships within the ruling classes of these three dynasties. Li Yuan not only held a position in the Sui dynasty but was also a cousin to Emperor Yang of Sui, Yang Guang.

In 617, seizing the opportunity amidst the chaos in the Sui Empire, Li Yuan, then the head of Hedong appointed by Emperor Yang of Sui, raised an army in Jinyang (present-day Taiyuan, Shanxi Province) and swiftly captured Chang'an and the surrounding Guanzhong region (present-day central Shaanxi Province). From there, he began his quest to unify China. In less than eight years, the Tang dynasty basically completed its unification, which was quite smooth and made possible by the achievements of the Sui dynasty.

Once in power, Li Yuan faced similar challenges to those encountered by Yang Jian in his time. Fortunately, his successor, Li Shimin, later known as Emperor Taizong of Tang (reigned 626–649), possessed a clear understanding and high vigilance regarding these issues. Learning from the mistakes of Emperor Yang of Sui, Li Shimin implemented a series of measures to stabilize the regime, thereby averting the recurrence of "perishing in the second generation." Emperor Taizong of Tang, renowned for his wisdom, is considered among the most illustrious rulers in ancient China and he was also good at whitewashing. Like Emperor Yang of Sui, Li Shimin was the second son of a founding emperor. At the age of eighteen, he joined his father's army and made remarkable military achievements during the establishment of the dynasty. According to the principle of primogeniture, his elder brother, Li Jiancheng, was the rightful heir to the throne. However,

Fig. 46 Salu Purple was one of the warhorses of Li Shimin, Emperor Taizong of Tang. In a battle near Luoyang, Henan Province, the emperor broke through with this horse, but it was struck by an arrow and was severely wounded. Upon returning, Li Shimin ordered the arrow to be removed. Salu Purple, showing loyalty and bravery, did not neigh, but slowly closed its eyes and died. This stone carving depicts the scene of removing the arrow. To honor the warhorse's brave act, the emperor ordered the depiction of the scene of arrow removal to be carved onto a stone screen.

Li Shimin, ambitious and resolute, ultimately eliminated Li Jiancheng and his other younger brother, Li Yuanji, through a palace coup, compelling his father, Li Yuan, to abdicate. Through these controversial methods, he ascended the throne.

Upon assuming power, Li Shimin tampered with historical records and greatly devalued the roles of his father and brothers. Consequently, contemporary historical accounts often portray him as the foremost figure in the founding of the dynasty, a portrayal that diverges from historical realities (fig. 46).

After his accession to the throne, Li Shimin implemented comparatively democratic governance methods, emphasizing collective decision-making and cultivating a positive interactive atmosphere within his court. It was during his reign of over twenty years that the administrative systems were formalized for the Tang Empire. Moreover, he vanquished the northern nomadic polity, the Eastern Turkic Khaganate (the Turkic Khaganate had splintered into Eastern and Western branches then), asserting dominance in East Asia. Subsequently, he began overseeing the Western Regions, roughly corresponding to present-day Xinjiang in northwestern China, and occasionally extending into parts of Central Asia. As a result, the emperors of the Tang Empire acquired the additional title of "Emperor and Khan," symbolizing their dual authority as supreme rulers over both the Central Plains and the northern steppes region.

3. The Only Empress

After the death of Li Shimin, his son, Li Zhi (reigned 649–683), assumed the throne. As Emperor Gaozong of Tang, he further expanded Tang's control over the Western Regions, defeating the Western Turkic Khaganate. With this victory, the Tang empire secured its dominance in Central Asia, signifying a period of increasing national strength. However, after Gaozong's reign, the Tang dynasty "perished" for a while and was replaced by the Zhou dynasty. Of course, this was not a revival of the previous Northern Zhou dynasty, but the Wuzhou dynasty, a regime established by Gaozong's wife, Empress Wu Zetian (624–705). The replacement of a dynasty at the height of its power by another is a relatively rare occurrence in history.

Wu Zetian hailed from a distinguished family with military accomplishments during the establishment of the Tang dynasty, although she was not affiliated with the Guanlong Military Aristocracy Group, from which the royal lineage originated. At the age of fourteen, she entered the palace as a low-ranking concubine of Emperor Taizong. After Emperor Taizong's passing, she followed tradition and became a nun, but Emperor Gaozong soon summoned her back to the palace, where her status gradually ascended, eventually leading to her coronation as empress. This elevation was achieved through arduous political struggles. Many former officials of Emperor Taizong, particularly those of the Guanlong Group, faced significant setbacks. Capitalizing on Emperor Gaozong's ailing health, Wu Zetian ventured into politics and, leveraging her exceptional political astuteness and unique historical circumstances, succeeded in establishing her own dynasty, thereby becoming the sole female empress in Chinese history.

Wu Zetian was an extraordinarily imaginative ruler, employing a diverse range of political tactics. As an unprecedented female empress, since traditional Chinese classics did not provide a legitimate basis for female rule, she turned to Buddhist scriptures, which depicted female rulers. Through intentional interpretation, Wu Zetian was considered akin to the celestial

maidens mentioned in Buddhist texts, believed to be the incarnation of Maitreya Buddha and thus destined to rule the empire. Proclaiming herself the Chakravartin, or world ruler in Buddhism traditions, she actively promoted Buddhism by ordering the translation of scriptures and the construction of temples throughout the empire. Today, the Longmen Grottoes in Luoyang still preserve many Buddhist statues commissioned by her (fig. 47).

However, the populace still longed for the former Tang dynasty. In the waning years of the Wuzhou era, certain ministers staged a coup, reinstalling Wu Zetian's son, Emperor Zhongzong of Tang (reigned 705–710, for the second time), and the Tang dynasty was then revived. After Wu Zetian's death, she was buried alongside her husband, Emperor Gaozong. What is even more remarkable is that, since the Qin and Han dynasties, every emperor and notable figure aspired to have their achievements memorialized for posterity. Yet, on the stone tablet of this sole legitimate empress in Chinese history, not a single word is inscribed, leaving endless speculation for future generations.

4. Song of Everlasting Regret

The era following the Tang dynasty's resurgence saw nearly a decade of upheaval. Eventually, one of Wu Zetian's grandsons, Li Longji, known as Emperor Xuanzong (reigned 712–756), ascended the throne through two palace coups. Xuanzong's reign lasted over forty years, making him the longest-reigning monarch of the Tang dynasty. During his rule, he instituted significant reforms to adapt to circumstances and improve governance efficiency, notably in the realms of finance and the military. For instance, he established specialized officials to oversee financial matters, implemented a military district system along the borders, and appointed jiedushi, a regional governor

Fig. 47 The Longmen Grottoes in Luoyang, Henan Province, is the world's largest and most extensive repository of stone carving art. The image above depicts the highly representative Great Vairocana Buddha, modeled after the likeness of Empress Wu Zetian.

Fig. 48 *Empress Yang Guifei Teaching a Parrot*

This mural comes from an ancient Liao dynasty (916–1125) tomb in Chifeng, Inner Mongolia Autonomous Region. It exhibits the typical style from the late Tang to the Five Dynasties period (907–960). In the painting, a woman with a high bun and adorned with golden hairpins looks elegant and noble as she gazes at a white parrot before her. Scholars speculate that this depicts Yang Guifei training a parrot.

with authority over military, administrative, and supervisory affairs, emphasizing specialization. These reforms ushered the Tang empire into a period of remarkable prosperity. Not only did its territorial expansion continue, firmly controlling the Western Regions and extending influence into Central Asia, but it also experienced economic affluence, with prices of essential goods like rice, flour, and silk remaining relatively low. The prosperity of the period is depicted in Tang dynasty poet Du Fu's (712–770) poem *Recalling the Past*:

I recall long ago when the Kaiyuan reign was in its glory days,

even small towns contained within homes of ten thousand families.

The rice flowed with oil, the millet was white,

granaries public and private both were filled with bounty.

What is even more renowned about Emperor Xuanzong of Tang is his love affair with Yang Guifei, a celebrated beauty of ancient China (fig. 48). Their tragic tale has echoed through the ages, immortalized in the Tang dynasty poet Bai Juyi's (772–846) *Chang Hen Ge* (also known as *Song of Everlasting Regret*). The line "In heaven, we wish to be two birds flying wing to wing; on earth, we wish to be two branches entwined together" from this poem has become a romantic pledge for countless couples expressing their lifelong devotion. However, the tragic catalyst was An Lushan, a non-Han jiedushi, who brought an end to the golden era of the Tang dynasty.

In AD 755, An Lushan, the jiedushi of Hebei Province (with its capital around present-day Beijing) rebelled, sparking the so-called An Lushan Rebellion, which lasted for eight years. This event marked a turning point not only for the Tang dynasty but also for Chinese history. Following this rebellion, China would lose control over the Western Regions for a long time, and the cosmopolitan character of the empire gradually faded away, shifting towards conservatism and internal control.

Back to our protagonists, Emperor Xuanzong and Yang Guifei. The reason why their love was a tragedy lies in the following. As An Lushan's forces approached the capital Chang'an, the royal family fled. Blaming Emperor Xuanzong's favoritism towards Yang Guifei's distant cousin, Yang Guozhong, and other members of the Yang family for the rebellion, the furious soldiers protecting the fleeing entourage threatened to abandon their loyalty when they reached Maweiyi in Xingping county if the emperor would not immediately execute the concubine. The 72-year-old emperor was left with no choice but to order Yang Guifei's execution to appease the soldiers' anger and ensure their safe escape. Eventually, the gorgeous beauty met her demise at the age of 38 about 50 kilometers west of the capital.

Epitomes of Cosmopolitanism

Modern historians often characterize the Sui and Tang dynasties as epitomes of cosmopolitanism. On the one hand, during their zenith before the An Lushan Rebellion, these empires expanded their territory far beyond the boundaries of the Han dynasty. They not only directly governed the Western Regions but also exerted influence beyond the natural barrier of the Pamir Plateau, extending into Central Asia. On the other hand, socio-culturally, these empires embraced a high degree of openness and tolerance, fostering inclusivity towards people, religions, arts, and cultures from diverse origins. Numerous foreign religions made their way into China, with Zoroastrianism, Manichaeism, and Nestorianism being particularly prominent. These foreign faiths brought diverse modes of thought and ideologies, along with Buddhism and Taoism, constituting the multifaceted belief system of the Tang dynasty.

I. The Evolving Regional Dynamics

The cosmopolitanism of the Tang Empire was intricately linked to the evolving regional dynamics of the time. Initially, the primary contenders against the Sui and Tang empires were the First and Second Turkic Khaganates, emerging from the northern steppes. They were followed by the unified Tibetan Regime on the Qinghai-Tibet Plateau in the west and the Uyghur Khaganate, which inherited Turkic dominance. By the late Tang period, the Nanzhao kingdom in the south and the Khitan in the northeast completed the process of statehood, adding further complexity to the geopolitical landscape. This cycle of emergence and decline among neighboring political entities compelled the Tang Empire to pursue an active foreign policy, particularly focusing on the Western Regions.

In the Tang dynasty, the Western Regions served as a crucial juncture for interactions between the Central Plains and Central Asia. Influenced by civilizations from the Central Plains, Persia, and India, it functioned as a crossroads of diverse religions and cultures, making it a target of competition for surrounding major powers. In essence, whichever regime controlled the Western Regions gained an advantage in balancing against other powers.

After defeating the Eastern Turkic Khaganate, Emperor Taizong redirected his attention to the Western Regions. In AD 658, he vanquished the Western Turkic Khaganate, bringing an end to their dominion in the Western Regions and integrating its territories into the Tang Empire. To ensure stable governance, the Tang dynasty introduced the same administrative systems as the inner prefectures and counties in the Western Regions, directly overseeing the territories. The most notable measure was the establishment of military garrisons, known

Fig. 49 Ancient Qiuci was the unique intersection of ancient Indian, Greek, Roman, Persian, and Han-Tang civilizations. Today, the Kizil Caves in Kuqa City, Xinjiang, are a highly significant cultural node on the Silk Road.

as the "Four Garrisons of Anxi," in Qiuci (fig. 49), Yanqi, Yutian, and Shule (present-day Kuqa City, southwestern Yanqi, southwestern Hetian, and Kashgar in Xinjiang). By the era of Emperor Xuanzong, Tang rule extended into Central Asia.

At the same time, the Arab Empire was expanding into Central Asia. In a highly coincidental turn of events, the two major empires of the world converged in Central Asia. In AD 750, they clashed in a decisive battle at Talas, with the Tang forces ultimately suffering defeat. This event is known as the "Battle of Talas." However, after the war, the Tang dynasty did not withdraw from Central Asia and still retained its suzerainty over the Central Asian countries.

The significant turning point came with the eruption of the An Lushan Rebellion, originating from the northeastern border of the empire, rapidly penetrating the imperial capitals of Luoyang and Chang'an, and forcing the imperial family to flee to Sichuan Province. In response to this large-scale military revolt, the Tang court had to mobilize a substantial portion of the northwest border troops, comparable in strength to those in the northeast, to quell the rebellion. The relocation of the armies stationed in the Western Regions to the Central Plains left the western border vulnerable. Seizing this opportunity, the Tibetan Regime expanded its control over vast territories in Longyou and Hexi (present-day Ningxia, Gansu, and Qinghai provinces in northwestern China). As the Tibetan Regime grew stronger, it extended its territory further eastward, establishing the Longshan and Helan mountains as the boundary with the Tang Empire. By the late 8th century, the Tang Empire had entirely relinquished control over the Western

Regions, leading to fierce competition between the Tibetan Regime and the Uyghur Khaganate for dominance in the region. However, Tang influence persisted in the Western Regions, with various systems and cultural legacies enduring for centuries.

2. Sogdians and An Lushan Rebellion

The An Lushan Rebellion had significant impacts on the Tang dynasty. Neither of its instigators, An Lushan and Shi Siming, were of Han Chinese descent. Both Sogdians, they were "foreigners" serving the Tang court. An Lushan was a Turkicized Sogdian, he exhibited traits typical of Sogdian merchants, including linguistic proficiency. Indeed, An Lushan's political trajectory notably benefited from his role as a translator for foreign trade along the northeastern border. Shi Siming shared a similar cultural and educational upbringing.

The Sogdians, renowned for their commercial acumen in Central Asia, cultivated a magnificent culture and dominated trade along the Silk Road. During the Sui and Tang dynasties, numerous Sogdians migrated to China. Adhering to Zoroastrianism, they were referred to as "Hu people" during the Tang dynasty and often settled in their own communities, forming distinct business networks. The Hu lifestyle, admired across all levels of society, left its mark on various facets of Tang culture, evident in clothing, cuisine, music, dance (see fig. 51 on pages 90–91), and sports.

Influenced by Hu culture, a more relaxed and friendly attitude towards women emerged, contributing to the reputation of Tang women for their independence, openness, and frankness (fig. 50). Moreover, owing to the Xianbei lineage of Tang rulers, they adopted an inclusive stance towards various tribes that submitted to their rule, including the Turks, Tuyuhun, Khitans, Tubo, and Uighurs. Consequently, the Tang Empire, particularly the city of Chang'an, flourished as an international hub where diverse ethnicities and religions coexisted, bustling with settlers and travelers. Along the border regions, large communities of diverse ethnic groups lived together. These foreign tribes attached to the Tang dynasty formed a crucial defense against adversaries from the steppes and served as the backbone of the Tang military in the eastern and western borderlands prior

Fig. 50 In the open and progressive Tang dynasty, women enjoyed a relatively free and open lifestyle. They were spirited, brave, carefree, and expressive in their personalities. Hu-style clothing was popular among them. Numerous female horse-riding figurines have been unearthed, depicting various activities such as spring outings, musical performances, hunting, and playing maqiu, a ball game like polo.

to the An Lushan Rebellion.

An Lushan, a Hu man, emerged during an era when Hu culture was prevalent. When he started his rebellion, many of its commanders were Sogdians, Turks, or Khitans. It is highly likely that An Lushan capitalized on their adherence to Zoroastrianism to secure their support. Their military prowess greatly bolstered the strength of the rebellion forces.

An Empire Transformed

From the An Lushan Rebellion to the fall of the Tang dynasty, a span of 150 years unfolded. Historically, the latter half of the dynasty has been perceived with oversimplification and negativity in both scholarly studies and popular understanding, as if this period, which spanned half of the entire Tang dynasty, was completely unrepresentative of the prosperous and splendid Tang Empire. The conventional perspective attributes the decline of the dynasty to court factionalism, the influence of eunuchs at the side of the monarch, and the growing power of provincial military governors.

The term "court factionalism" refers to a forty-year power struggle between two factions within the court during the first half of the 9th century. Eunuchs colluded with court ministers, involving themselves in daily political operations and exerting influence over the imperial guards and the enthronement of emperors. On the other hand, the jiedushi system granted significant political and military authority to provincial military governors, posing a challenge to the central government's authority.

The stereotype, largely perpetuated by

Fig. 51　Mural of Cave 220 at the Mogao Grottoes (detail)

Tang dynasty

The Sogdian Whirl was the most popular ethnic dance during the Tang dynasty, characterized by rapid spinning and swirling to the left and right. In this part of the mural from the Mogao Grottoes in Dunhuang, the two dancers on the left elegantly move with the Sogdian Whirl on small round carpets.

historical records, has become so ingrained that it has led to the oversight of more pivotal reforms, some of which were revolutionary.

I. Keju and the Literati

From the perspective of the ruling class, the latter half of the Tang dynasty witnessed a crucial transition from an aristocratic to a commoner society. In the early Tang period, feudalistic concepts inherited from the Southern and Northern dynasties still prevailed, and the Guanlong Aristocratic Group constituted the main source of senior officials. However, starting from Empress Wu Zetian, this situation gradually changed. To consolidate her power, she introduced reforms in the keju system, a system for selecting officials through civil service examinations which originated in the Sui dynasty, allowing people from humble backgrounds to enter the political elite. By the late Tang period, the imperial examination system had become the primary means of selecting officials. The criterion of the selection was literary talent, rather than the previous criteria based on nobility. This unprecedented change allowed commoners the opportunity to enter the political core of the dynasty, leading to a reconstruction of all levels of social strata. At the same time, the new system of selecting officials facilitated a shift towards emphasizing literacy over military skill, resulting in a peak in literature and establishing a tradition of prioritizing literary pursuits.

During a certain period, there were instances where influential families manipulated the imperial examination system, using it as a vital means to uphold their status and secure high-ranking positions. These families, dominant in the examination process, emerged as the new "nobility." However, unlike the past, the criteria for this new elite were not solely based on lineage and ancestry but rather on examination performance. This shift can be viewed as a form of progress compared to earlier times.

2. System of Eunuchs

Eunuchs in the late Tang period also had many special characteristics. Whether in ancient Asia or Europe, eunuch involvement in politics was a common phenomenon. From the ancient Assyrian Empire to the Roman Empire and Byzantium, eunuchs were considered the most trustworthy of servants due to their special access to the inner chambers of the palace without the threat of uniting the heirs to establish a rival dynasty. However, historical records often dwarfed and discriminated against them.

Eunuchs in the late Tang period differed from those in earlier times when they primarily came from humble backgrounds, such as war captives from remote southern areas. Instead, many of them were from lower-ranking official families near the capital. They often possessed higher levels of literacy, and their duties and evaluations were not significantly different from those of regular officials. For instance, they served as military supervisors in regional garrisons, working alongside and overseeing local military governors. At times, they acted as special envoys representing the emperor, playing a crucial role in bridging the gap between the inner palace and other governmental functions of the empire (fig. 52).

Fig. 52 White Glazed Head of a Eunuch Figurine
Tang dynasty
Qianling Museum, Xianyang, Shaanxi Province
This figurine has a clean-shaven face without a mustache, with furrowed brows and a stern expression, exuding an air of authority. It portrays the image of a high-ranking eunuch from the Tang dynasty.

3. Provincial Military Commissions

The An Lushan Rebellion was instigated by An Lushan and Shi Siming, both serving as commanders of provincial military commissions. However, far from being disbanded, more of these regional military units were instituted throughout the empire. The provincial military commissions held substantial military and administrative authority, evolving into administrative bodies that bridged the central government and the administrations at the county level. At the same time, their power surpassed that of previous local institutions and displayed a distinct militaristic character.

At first glance, it appeared that China had reverted to an era of regional warlords. Yet, from a spatial point of view, military governors across different regions had varied relationships with the imperial court. For instance, the Hebei commission maintained a relatively autonomous stance for a prolonged period, while those in the west defended against external ethnic regimes. Some in the southeast contributed financial resources to the empire, and the Henan commission safeguarded the empire's transportation routes. Together, they played crucial roles in governing the empire.

Even the Hebei commission, which was the most independent and inherited the rebellious mantle of An Lushan, had to leverage the Tang dynasty's authority to maintain control and defend the empire against northeastern ethnic groups. Over time, nearly all military commissions aligned themselves with the central government, with fewer instances of defiance.

In summary, despite the apparent decline of the late Tang period, the authority of the court and the emperor were significantly strengthened. This is evidenced by the empire's ability to endure for another 150 years despite internal uprisings and challenges from regional military governors. In the context of Chinese history, this endurance is quite remarkable. China was operating with a more sophisticated and intricate system that effectively coordinated resources and various powers across the regions.

Tang Poetry

Aligned with economic prosperity, cultural progress reached its zenith during the Sui and Tang periods, leaving behind a rich legacy of renowned literary, painting, and calligraphic works. Among the well-known figures were poets Wang Wei (701?–761), Du Fu (712–770),

Li Bai (701–762), Bai Juyi (772–846), and Li Shangyin (813–858), calligraphers Yan Zhenqing (709–784) and Liu Gongquan (778–865), painters Yan Liben (601–673) and Wu Daozi (680–759), and essayists Han Yu (768–824) and Liu Zongyuan (773–819). However, if one were to pinpoint the cultural aspect that best represents this era, it would be Tang poetry. Although China boasts a longstanding tradition of poetry writing, the Tang dynasty stood as its golden age. Even today, Chinese school children are taught to appreciate and recite Tang poems.

The era of Emperor Xuanzong marked the zenith of Tang poetry, giving rise to the greatest poets Li Bai and Du Fu. Li Bai was born in the Western Regions but raised in Sichuan since childhood, and Du Fu hailed from a family of lower-ranking officials. Being ten years older, Li Bai gained fame much earlier than Du Fu, but neither of them achieved success in officialdom. However, Li Bai, financially comfortable and free-spirited, enjoyed drinking and traveling. With his bold and unrestrained personality, Li Bai produced numerous imaginative works, becoming the epitome of the vibrant Tang dynasty spirit. Du Fu, an admirer of Li Bai, depicted him vividly in one of his poems:

"Li Bai, with a jug of wine, writes a hundred poems,

Sleeping in taverns of Chang'an city, wherever he roams.

Imperial summons absolutely he'd decline,

Declaring himself the Immortal of Wine."

In contrast, Du Fu wasn't as fortunate. Despite multiple attempts, he failed to succeed in the imperial examinations for an official position. Although he later held minor governmental roles, he lived a life of instability and financial hardship. While both Li Bai and Du Fu experienced the tumultuous period of the An Lushan Rebellion, Li Bai passed away soon after, but Du Fu endured the entirety of the war and its aftermath, resulting in many of his works reflecting the realities of society and

the struggles of the lower class people. He is often described as a poet-historian.

A prominent poet from the later Tang dynasty was Bai Juyi, who thrived in the early 9th century. Unlike Li Bai and Du Fu, Bai Juyi enjoyed a relatively tranquil life, characterized by his serene and non-confrontational demeanor. His poetry covered a broad spectrum of topics, striking a balance between clarity and emotional depth, which resonated with a wide audience. Bai Juyi's accessible writing style attracted a large readership, and it is said that his works became so popular that common merchants even produced printed copies of his poems for sale. His influence extended far beyond the Tang dynasty, reaching neighboring regions like Silla in the Korean Peninsula and Japan, where it left a profound mark on Japanese literature.

Poetry flourished during the Tang dynasty in part due to the open and inclusive culture of the Sui and Tang empires, where diverse ideas, civilizations, religions, and people converged. Another significant factor was the imperial examination system, known as the keju, which included poetry writing as a subject. Consequently, the genre extended beyond its traditional boundaries to become a skill shared and valued by the ruling class, contributing to a society that highly esteemed literature.

The Legacy of the Tang Empire

The Tang Empire met its demise due to the Huang Chao Rebellion, a massive peasant uprising that engulfed nearly half of its territory. By that time, the imperial court was losing control over more regions, leading to the rise of local military leaders who rose to power during the suppression of the Huang Chao Rebellion and took control of the localities, and the provincial military commissions thus became de facto independent. In AD 907, Zhu Wen (reigned 907–912), a leader from the Henan military commission who had previously been associated with the Huang Chao army and later surrendered to the Tang, assassinated the Tang emperor, whom he had abducted, after he ruthlessly purged eunuchs and high-ranking civil officials from the Tang court. Seizing the throne, he established the Later

Fig. 53 Mural of Cave 220 at the Mogao Grottoes. Please refer to fig. 51 on pages 90–91 for more information.

Liang dynasty (907–923), effectively bringing an end to the Tang dynasty.

The period from the fall of the Tang dynasty to the subsequent reunification under the Northern Song dynasty (960–1126) is commonly known as the Five Dynasties and Ten Kingdoms period (907–979). In the north, five dynasties—Liang, Tang, Jin, Han, and Zhou—successively emerged in the Central Plains, while nine concurrent regimes were established in southern China. Additionally, during the later stages of the Five Dynasties (907–960), the Northern Han ruled over parts of the Hedong region (present-day Shanxi Province), leading to the designation of "Ten Kingdoms (902–979)."

This era lasted approximately eighty years, significantly shorter than the four hundred years of division following the collapse of the Qin and Han dynasties. The brevity of this division can be attributed to the large-scale infrastructure projects undertaken during the Sui and Tang dynasties to unify the empire. For example, the construction of the Grand Canal, linking Chang'an city with southeastern China, facilitated further integration between the northern and southern regions of the empire. Thus, the division during the Five Dynasties and Ten Kingdoms era was not merely a repetition of past conflicts between the north and south.

The Five Dynasties and Ten Kingdoms period was an era of fragmentation, but it was not without benefits for local regions. To maintain the survival of their regimes, the regional rulers adopted various methods to boost local economies. The southern states promoted trading with foreign countries, laying the foundation for the development of the Maritime Silk Road (the network of sea routes that link the East with the West) along the southeastern coast in the period after the Song dynasty (960–1279). It was during this period that the economic center of ancient China further shifted southward.

While the Tang Empire collapsed, its influence persisted. The imperial title was maintained, though intermittently, for nearly half a century in two regimes of the Five Dynasties and Ten Kingdoms. More importantly, the political heritage and institutional system of the Tang were further developed and eventually integrated into the Northern Song dynasty.

CHAPTER SIX
Governing with Scholar Officials: The Song Dynasty

Amidst the chaos of the An Lushan Rebellion and the discord among regional warlords, military governance emerged as a daunting obstacle to the aristocratic norms spanning from the late Han to the Tang dynasty. Ostensibly, local warlords, frequently ascending from humble origins in the lower ranks, commanded considerable authority within their domains, directly contesting the central aristocratic order. Yet, internally, these regional military factions encompassed numerous literati who lacked noble lineage. The framework of clan-centric politics, built on familial bonds and aristocratic lineage, ultimately disintegrated under the growing sway of individuals from modest beginnings.

The profound shifts in political dynamics were punctuated by brutal violence. Amidst the struggle for supremacy among local warlords, military generals emerged as key political players. In the turbulent power struggles of the late Tang and Five Dynasties period, Zhao Kuangyin (927–976), a general of the Later Zhou dynasty, instigated a military coup in 960. Commanding his followers to dress him in imperial yellow robes and proclaim him emperor, he seized the Later Zhou regime and established the Song dynasty. From 963 to 979, the Song military quelled various separatist factions, heralding the conclusion of the fractured China of the Five Dynasties and Ten Kingdoms era. The new dynasty presented a demeanor significantly distinct from the preceding chaotic era.

Ambitious Scholar-Officials

Seizing power through military means himself, Zhao Kuangyin (reigned 960–976), posthumously known as Emperor Taizu of Song (fig. 54), astutely recognized the potential threat posed by military generals to his imperial authority. Shortly after consolidating his rule, he began to seize the armies of the local warlords to diminish their power. Concurrently, he invited the general officers who had aided his ascent to a lavish banquet, where he negotiated with them, persuading them to surrender their military commands in exchange for honorary titles, comfortable government positions, and generous pensions. Consequently, during the successive reigns of Taizu and his brother, Emperor Taizong (reigned 976–997), a groundbreaking system of civil governance, with large-scale imperial examinations to identify and elevate talented individuals, was established. The literati, once overshadowed by military figures yet pivotal in dismantling the previous clan-based politics, emerged as significant political figures. With civil officials assuming prominent roles and receiving preferential treatment, the Song dynasty prioritized civil administration over military prowess.

On the facing page
Fig. 54 This is a portrait of Zhao Kuangyin, Emperor Taizu of Song, from the National Museum of China, Beijing.

I. Imperial Examination for All

Departing from clan-based politics, the Song dynasty placed significant reliance on the imperial examination system (keju) for the selection of civil officials. Virtually all major roles within significant government departments mandated candidates to have attained the prestigious title of jinshi, the highest and final degree in the imperial examination conducted in the capital. Should the emperor wish to appoint an individual lacking the jinshi title to a prominent position, he had to devise means to confer the title upon them beforehand, or else he was bound to incur criticism and opposition from his ministers.

Of course, keju was not the only way for the Song people to find a way into an official career. There were also bureaucrats hailing from influential families who could still secure official positions by virtue of their grandparents or parents holding high offices, which used to be the most common practice for the ruling group to replace the fresh blood in the clan-based political era. However, during the Song dynasty, such appointments were generally relegated to lower-level positions, and the path to advancement was challenging for these officials. The Song government's personnel system prioritized the promotion of candidates who had successfully passed the imperial examinations, ensuring governance by the educated class.

Under the reign of Emperor Renzong (reigned 1022–1063), a system was introduced wherein, among candidates with equal scores, commoner examinees were given preference over those from privileged backgrounds. Interestingly, upon the announcement of imperial examination results, high-ranking officials and wealthy merchants eagerly sought to arrange marriages between the newly appointed jinshi and members of their families.

The Song dynasty's imperial examination system, open to all social strata, was fiercely competitive. Those who ultimately obtained the qualification of jinshi were truly exceptional individuals. Nevertheless, this system provided the

Fig. 55 A painting from the Northern Song dynasty (960–1126) depicting the grand scene of the emperor leaving the city to perform a ritual offering to Heaven and Earth. It shows the appearance of civil officials during the period.

populace with relatively fair opportunities to move up the hierarchy, establishing a mechanism for social mobility. Influential families could no longer monopolize high positions for generations, and commoners with unprivileged backgrounds could excel through education, thereby refreshing and enhancing the overall quality of the civil servant class (fig. 55).

2. Scholars with State Concerns

Many revered statesmen of the Song dynasty rose from humble beginnings. Consider Fan Zhongyan (989–1052), a philosopher and poet, who served as Prime Minister to Emperor Renzong. He lost his father at age two and was raised by his struggling mother, who later remarried. During his youth, he studied in a mountain monastery, sustaining himself on little more than a small bowl of porridge each day. Despite these hardships, he excelled in the imperial examinations and entered government service. Even in his early days as a minor official in the highest court, his annual salary equaled the income from two thousand acres of land. Fan Zhongyan, who ascended in social status, often pondered "how to repay the country's kindness." Many scholars from similar backgrounds shared his sense of gratitude.

In this atmosphere, the purpose of education had evolved beyond leisure and refinement to the ambition of bettering the county. Scholars immersed themselves not only in politics and governance but also in documenting their political and academic ideals, to be passed down to future generations. Practical administrative experience was highly valued; Emperor Taizong convened relevant officials to consult on fiscal matters and solutions. He emphasized that high officials proficient in rhetoric should not hesitate to seek advice and guidance from professionals on specific issues. Consequently, books detailing

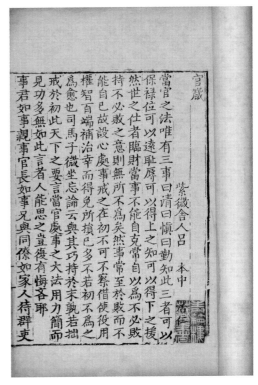

Fig. 56 An image of a book from the Northern Song dynasty that describes the principles of being an official and administrative experiences.

governance and administrative experiences became popular, emphasizing minute practicalities and possessing strong guiding and actionable qualities (fig. 56).

In contrast to the clan-based aristocratic era, where power was shared between noble families and the emperor, now in the Song dynasty, well-read scholars, regardless of their background, assisted the emperor in governing the nation. The high-spirited scholars, both within and outside official circles, exuded immense confidence. Some who grasped the intricacies of imperial governance even counseled the emperor against excessive interference in specific administrative matters. Scholars nationwide adhered to their ideals of "understanding the essence of issues, pursuing knowledge, nurturing integrity, fostering sincerity, maintaining family harmony, engaging in state affairs, and striving for global peace."

A Trio of Confucianism, Buddhism, and Taoism

The Song dynasty, established through military usurpation, avoided repeating the mistakes of its predecessors by diminishing the authority of military generals and prioritizing civilian governance. However, being a dynasty founded through military means, it still faced the challenge of reestablishing state authority and ideological order after breaking down the clan-based politics. Since the reign of Emperor Wu of the Han dynasty, Confucianism had been upheld as the orthodox ideology. However, thereafter, Confucianism, Buddhism, and Taoism competed in the ideological arena. During the Wei and Jin dynasties, Taoist discourse on metaphysics flourished, while Buddhism experienced significant growth during the Sui and Tang dynasties. Against the backdrop of the strengths of Confucianism, Buddhism (fig. 57), and Taoism, profound integration and transformation occurred in the ideological landscape of the Song dynasty.

I. The Rise of Zen

After flourishing during the Tang dynasty, Buddhism, a foreign religion, gave rise to the indigenous Zen sect in China. Disregarding scriptures, doctrines, and rituals, Zen Buddhists believed that all truth, goodness, and beauty reside within one's own nature,

On the facing page

Fig. 57 Colored Wooden Carving of Seated Guanyin Bodhisattva

Song dynasty
Height 200 cm
National Museum of China, Beijing

Wooden carvings reached their peak during the Song dynasty, with exceptional achievements in the art of Bodhisattva statues. This seated statue of Guanyin presents a gentle and compassionate female figure, imbued with serene beauty within its solemnity, reflecting the aesthetic spirit of the period.

the recognition of which could lead to self-enlightenment and self-liberation. Instead of adhering to the traditional Buddhist practices of asceticism, Zen Buddhism emphasized instantaneous intuitive understanding as the way to cognize one's own nature. To inspire disciples to enlightenment, Zen masters often used profound words or actions known as "jifeng," literally meaning the nock point on the bow and the tip of the arrow, guiding disciples to a new understanding of their nature. For example, a starving disciple would be offered a bowl of porridge. When he is about to eat, the food is taken away and smashed on the ground, and he is then asked, "Do you still need the porridge?" This unexpected act, which seems to be irrational but is full of philosophy, aimed to break disciples' habitual logic and lead them to insight into their own nature (see fig. 58 on page 102).

Many Confucian scholars, well-versed in classical texts, were drawn to the Zen teaching method, engaging closely with Zen monks to exchange views on wisdom and human nature. Ouyang Xiu (1007–1072), a historian, calligrapher, epigrapher, essayist, poet, and prominent Confucian scholar of the Song dynasty, initially saw his mission as reviving Confucianism and viewed Buddhism as a demonic religion. However, after interacting with Zen monks, he felt relieved and was so impressed that he turned to study and practice Zen Buddhism. In his later years, Ouyang Xiu adopted the self-title "Liu Yi Jushi," with "Jushi" denoting a lay Buddhist practitioner.

The engagement of scholars in Zen Buddhism during the Song dynasty also spurred changes within the Zen tradition itself. Initially, Zen Buddhist principles were seldom recorded in writing, but scholars adept in writing encouraged Zen monks to articulate and advocate Zen teachings through words. Numerous texts documenting the lineages of various Zen schools and the sayings of Zen masters,

known as "records of the lamp's transmission" (chuan deng lu), were compiled during this era. The "lamp" serves as a metaphor for Zen teachings, representing their capacity to illuminate the darkness of human nature. "Transmission" refers to the passing on of the lamp, symbolizing the perpetuation and dissemination of Zen teachings. The writing style of these texts reflects the philosophical expressions of Zen masters, characterized by simplicity and vividness, appealing to both the refined and the common people.

2. The Birth of Neo-Confucianism

While Buddhism gained popularity for its karmic and salvational ideology and Zen sects won the favor of scholars with their incisive wisdom, metaphysical studies since the Wei and Jin dynasties were known for their speculation of transcendental issues. In contrast, Confucianist teachings, with their straightforward moral precepts and utilitarian political discourse, lack exploration of ultimate questions. Confucian scholars primarily focused on annotating and interpreting Confucian classics, lacking a rigorous theoretical framework. As a result, it faced competition with Buddhism and Taoism. Confucianism, as the official doctrine, was marginalized and several Song emperors turned to Buddhism or Taoism. Emperor Zhenzong (reigned 998–1022) chose Taoism to mythologize the rule of his family, depicting his ancestors as Taoist immortals. Similarly, Emperor Huizong (reigned 1100–

On the facing page
Fig. 58 *The Sixth Patriarch Tearing the Sutra*
Liang Kai (c. 1140–1210)
Ink on paper
Length 30.3 cm, height 70 cm
Mitsui Memorial Museum, Tokyo

This painting depicts Master Huineng, the Sixth Patriarch, holding a sutra that he has torn apart, in a scene of rapid steps and frenzied shouts. The use of dry and rough ink strokes portrays the master's irreverent attitude towards worldly matters.

1126) even referred to himself as the "supreme emperor of the Taoist master." When the Jin army approached the capital, he even hoped that Taoist sorcery could repel the invaders.

In this context, scholars who were well-versed in Confucian classics and entered governance through the imperial examination system became discontent with being merely perceived by the monarchy as utilitarian administrators. They wanted to be the guardians of Confucian culture and sought to revive Confucianism to reconstruct the ideological order of the nation. This coincided with the pragmatic consideration of the government to establish state authority in the realm of ideology. Under the joint impetus of both practicality and ideal, Confucianism underwent introspection and transformation and began to evolve into "lixue" (School of Universal Principles), or Neo-Confucianism.

Classic Confucianism primarily focuses on human ethics, neglecting discussions on ultimate issues such as cosmology, which are emphasized by Buddhism and Taoism. Drawing upon the metaphysical strengths of these two philosophies, Neo-Confucianists expanded their inquiries beyond moral principles to encompass all aspects of the universe, creating a framework that integrates views on cosmology, society, and human life. This ideological system offered comprehensive solutions for reconstructing and unifying state authority and ideological order. However, these solutions, devised by Song scholar-officials who ruled the country together with the emperor, aiming to safeguard cultural values, sometimes challenged imperial authority. Their ultimate ideal, articulated by Song philosopher and politician Zhang Zai (1020–1077), "ordaining conscience for Heaven and Earth, securing life and fortune for the people, continuing lost teachings for past sages, and establishing peace for all future generations," left no room for imperial authority and inevitably provoked resistance from imperial rulers.

3. Imperial Neo-Confucianism

The Song emperors continued to bolster imperial authority. During the Tang and Five Dynasties periods, ministers of scholarly background were granted seats when they met the emperor. After discussions, the emperor would conclude the audience by offering tea. However, beginning with Emperor Taizu of the Song, this protocol was abolished, and ministers were required to stand respectfully before the emperor, who held full authority. The Song emperors favored literary officials and scholars to prevent military officials from seizing power. Their focus on rebuilding ideological order and clarifying state authority aimed to underscore the emperor's supreme authority.

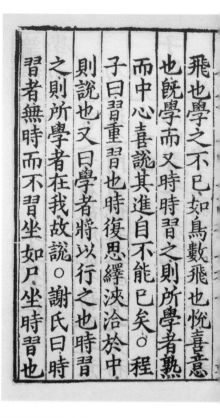

Fig. 59 *The Annotated Collection of The Analects of Confucius* by Zhu Xi.

In the early years of the Southern Song dynasty (1127–1276), Zhu Xi (1130–1200), a Chinese calligrapher, historian, philosopher, poet, and politician, summarized and integrated the Neo-Confucian thoughts of the Northern Song, becoming a leading master in that philosophy with a large group of disciples (figs. 59–60). However, Neo-Confucianism was marginalized after Emperor Ningzong (reigned 1194–1224) ascended the throne. It wasn't until the reign of Emperor Lizong (reigned 1224–1264) that the philosophical school was officially designated as the state ideology, and was recognized and honored as a new resource for the ruling ideology of the country. Posthumous honors were conferred by the court to Zhu Xi and others who had passed away by then. The temple name of Emperor Lizong was even derived from his reverence for Neo-Confucianism.

From being denounced as pseudo-learning to being revered as official philosophy, Neo-Confucianism once held the promise of standing at the pinnacle of ideology, guiding political and social operations, including those of imperial

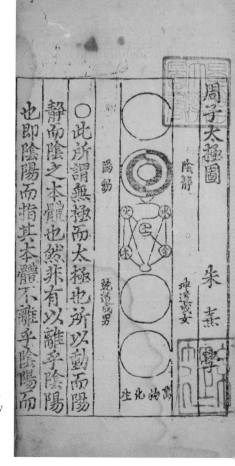

Fig. 60 Diagram of the universe by Neo-Confucian scholars of the Song dynasty.

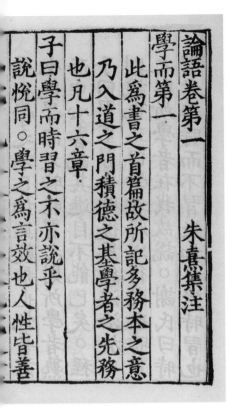

authority. However, it ultimately became little more than a tool of compliance for the imperial authority, simply affirming the emperor's possession of the "principle" to govern all matters and thus legitimizing imperial rule. In essence, it dictated that no one could use "principle" as a tool to meddle in imperial affairs. Faced with the autocracy of imperial authority, scholars of the Southern Song dynasty turned to self-preservation, no longer embodying the forthrightness and vigor of their counterparts in the Northern Song dynasty.

Local Economic Initiatives

Disheartened by their lack of influence on national affairs, scholars transitioned to roles as local gentry, devoting themselves to the advancement of their local communities. They minded the world, and although they could not achieve their ambitions at the imperial court, they could benefit their hometowns. This change resonated with the practical demands stemming from the societal shifts in the Song dynasty.

1. Officials as Local Gentry

Unlike Tang dynasty's land allocation system, which was based on population, the Song dynasty did not suppress land consolidation and allowed for the transfer of land ownership, determined by market demand. Consequently, some landlords accumulated vast amounts of land, with the state levying taxes based on land area. Generous bureaucratic salaries and tax-exempt land quotas privileged those in official positions in land consolidation. Wealthy merchants and usurers preferred to invest their capital in land after making profits. As a result, land titles were frequently transferred, often to a minority of owners, during the Song dynasty. Many small farmers lost their plots of land and became tenants renting land from landlords, leading to a series of social problems. The peasant uprisings during the Northern Song period were provoked in the name of wealth equalization. One of the core measures of the reforms carried out by Wang Anshi (1021–1086), a Chinese economist, philosopher, poet, and politician, was to equalize land taxes. While land consolidation and wealth disparity in the Southern Song period exceeded that of the Northern Song, there was no large-scale rural unrest on the whole. This was largely due to the coordination of rural socioeconomic relations by scholars acting as local gentry, contributing significantly to maintaining stability in grassroots society.

The local gentry, anchored in villages by blood ties or geographical affiliations, manifested their ideals of self-cultivation, family harmony, state governance, and world peace through local initiatives. They established community granaries and benevolent organizations to aid impoverished villagers, reconcile class disparities, and thus mitigate grassroots instability. Transitioning between the court and their hometowns, the scholar-officials of the Northern Song dynasty were dedicated to their principles. After enduring three demotions, Fan

Fig. 61 Image of Fan Zhongyan's relief efforts for his clan in Qing dynasty (1644–1911) literature.

Zhongyan returned to his hometown of Suzhou to found the Fan Family Benevolent Society, providing assistance to the impoverished clan members (fig. 61).

Such actions became increasingly common as Southern Song scholar-officials turned towards introspection and restraint. Instead of seeking higher official positions outside their villages, many of them began to focus on their immediate localities. For instance,

gatherings among fellow villagers in the capital city became increasingly significant for scholars, whether or not they held official duties. Due to military pressure from northern regimes, the economic growth of the Song dynasty heavily depended on the development of the hills and wetlands in the south. Originally unsuitable for agriculture, these areas were transformed into fertile lands through the construction and maintenance of water conservancy facilities such as reservoirs, embankments, and irrigation canals and ditches. It was often the local gentry who served as the core organizers of these construction projects and the maintainers of water usage order (fig. 62).

2. Prosperous Markets

Cities prior to the Song dynasty were primarily constructed as military fortresses for the ruler's defense, with markets serving as an accessory part of the fortress. Chang'an City, the capital of the Tang dynasty (modern-day Xi'an, Shaanxi Province), boasted a sizable population, vast size, and orderly layout. Residents resided within closed-off neighborhoods, and commercial transactions mainly occurred in two markets located at the eastern and western extremities of the city. Residents were permitted to leave their neighborhoods for shopping activities only between sunrise and sunset, signified by the sound of drums and gongs. The layout and

Fig. 62 Mulanbei in Putian City, Fujian Province. First built in 1064, it is one of China's most intact ancient irrigation projects still in existence.

governance of local cities typically mirrored that of Chang'an but on a smaller scale.

The cities in early Tang were divided into enclosed neighborhoods known as "fang." However, starting from the mid-Tang period, shops gradually began to break through the spatial limitations of the markets and fangs. By the Song dynasty, cities had transformed into bustling streets lined with shops, marking the shift to open street spaces as the primary spatial units. *The Eastern Capital: A Dream of Splendor*, a memoir written by essayist Meng Yuanlao (c. 1090–1150), provides a detailed description of the busy streets with various businesses in the capital city of Dongjing (present-day Kaifeng, Henan Province) during the late Northern Song period. Song painter Zhang Zeduan's (1085–

1145) scroll painting *Along the River During the Qingming Festival* is a visually striking portrayal of the urban landscape and the daily lives of commoners during the same period (fig. 63). In Song dynasty cities, the trading hours of shops were no longer restricted, and

Fig. 63 *Along the River During the Qingming Festival* (detail)
Zhang Zeduan (1085–1145)
Ink and color on silk
Length 528.7 cm, height 24.8 cm
The Palace Museum, Beijing

This work depicts the urban landscape and daily life of people from various social classes in the capital city of Dongjing during the Northern Song dynasty in the 12th century. Spanning over five meters, the scroll portrays a vast array of colorful figures, livestock including cows, mules, and donkeys, various vehicles including carts, sedan chairs, and boats of different sizes, as well as buildings, bridges, and city towers. It serves as a vivid testament to the prosperity of the capital city during the period. A close-up of the painting will be found on pages 108–109.

night markets became commonplace. Song official Cai Tao (1096–1162) describes the bustling night markets of the Song period in his literary sketches *Talks at Tieweishan*, stating that a street named Maxing in Dongjing was free from the annoyance of mosquitoes on summer nights because it was so busy with taverns and people that the mosquitoes disappeared due to the smoke from cooking oils.

Faced with military pressure from the northern regimes, the Southern Song dynasty moved its capital to Lin'an (present-day Hangzhou, Zhejiang Province), situated in the economically vibrant region of South China (fig. 64). The bustling scenes of the former capital, Dongjing, were quickly recreated in the new capital. This remarkable similarity to the pomp and splendor of the past era stirred feelings of anxiety and nostalgia in a patriotic poet, as expressed in his verse:

"The warm breeze intoxicates the travelers, mistaking Hangzhou for Dongjing."

However, from another perspective, the strong economy of the Song dynasty necessitated the establishment of such an open and vibrant urban center, a feat it had the capability to achieve.

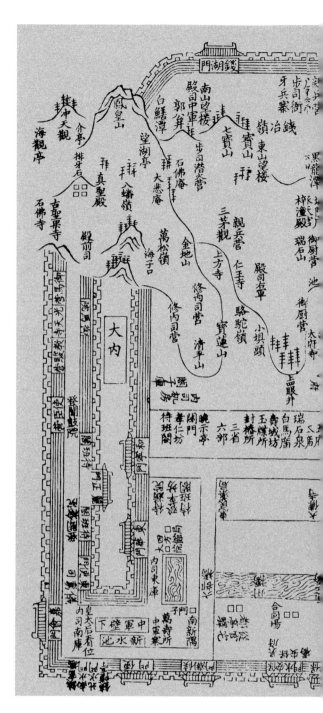

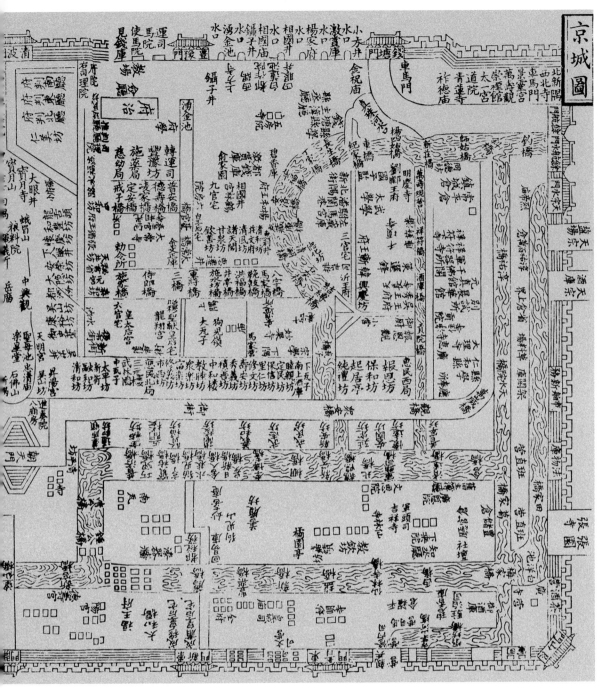

京城圖

Fig. 64 *The Map of the Capital City*, created in the Southern Song dynasty (1127–1276), depicting the layout of Lin'an (present-day Hangzhou, Zhejiang Province).

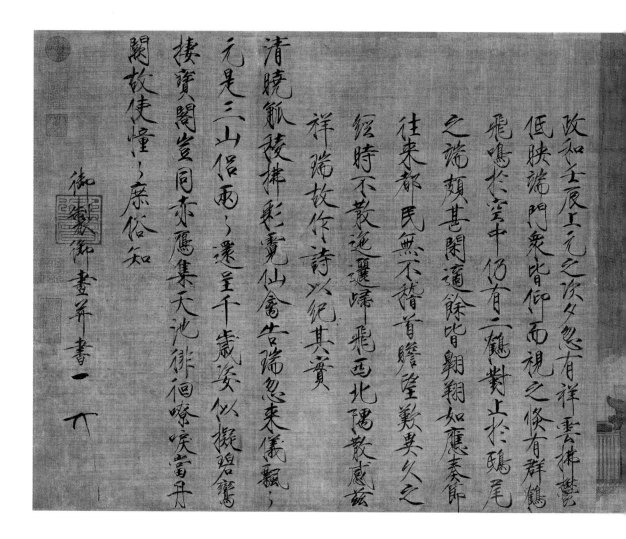

3. Song-Style Painting and Calligraphy

The Song dynasty marked the zenith of court painting in Chinese history. *Along the River During the Qingming Festival*, a masterpiece of realism by the court painter Zhang Zeduan, provides a vibrant depiction of daily life and the urban landscape of Dongjing during the Northern Song period. Revered for its realism, this painting inspired numerous replicas by artists of subsequent dynasties. Several Song emperors themselves were practitioners of the art form, actively fostering its development by recruiting talented artists for the court academies. Emperor Huizong of Song, in particular, not only curated renowned artworks but also showcased exceptional skills in calligraphy and painting.

He pioneered the "slender gold script," characterized by slender, vigorous strokes and powerful transitions at the beginning and end of each stroke, reflecting his distinctive artistic flair. In his paintings, the emperor displayed a particular affinity for flowers and birds, showcasing meticulous brushwork and a sense of opulence (fig. 65). With a commitment to realism, he captured the nuanced details of petals and leaves in depictions of Chinese roses across different seasons and times of day. Additionally, Emperor Huizong of Song established painting schools to nurture artistic talents, offering comprehensive courses in figure painting, landscape painting, and flower and bird painting, thereby laying the groundwork for various traditional Chinese painting genres.

Fig. 65 *Auspicious Cranes*
Zhao Ji (1082–1135, i.e., Emperor Huizong of Song dynasty)
Ink and color on silk
Length 138.2 cm, height 51 cm
Liaoning Provincial Museum

In this painting, the imperial palace is depicted majestically at the bottom, with cranes dancing in the deep blue sky above the palace, creating an atmosphere rich in auspicious and mystical qualities. On the left side is a poem inscribed in Emperor Huizong's unique slender gold script.

During the Song dynasty, celebrated for its lifelike court paintings, scholars pioneered what became known as "literati painting." This style captivated Song scholars, esteemed for their social standing, who avidly collected renowned artworks. Many scholars also honed their painting skills, using this art form as a medium to convey their emotions and sentiments. Literati paintings typically depicted landscapes, bamboo, rocks, flowers, and birds, with a profound emphasis on the expressive potential of ink wash techniques. Artists mastered the manipulation of ink density to evoke a range of emotions (see fig. 66 on pages 114–115). In contrast to the realistic approach favored by court painters, literati paintings prioritized conveying artistic concepts and pursued simplicity and elegance,

believed to be more emotionally resonant than the works of professional craftsmen. Su Shi (1037–1101), a distinguished Song poet, essayist, and painter, famously remarked that paintings focused solely on resemblance were akin to doodles made by a toddler.

Scholars also incorporated calligraphy into paintings, inscribing poems on their artworks, thereby significantly enhancing the expressive power of the art form.

Fig. 66 *Cloudy Mountains* (detail)
Mi Youren (1074–1153)
Ink and color on silk
Length 646.8 cm, height 45.5 cm
The Cleveland Museum of Art

In this painting, white clouds weave through the lush peaks and valleys, extending endlessly from left to right into the distant sky. The brushwork technique is highly stylized, featuring ink dots to depict branches, bridges, and boats. Despite its seemingly understated and misty appearance, it embodies the aesthetic charm of Song dynasty literati painting.

Concurrently, calligraphy among Song scholars developed its own distinctive traits. While Tang dynasty calligraphers emphasized adherence to writing principles and norms, their counterparts in the Song dynasty revered artistic conception, seeking to transcend established rules and norms to express originality. This new dimension of Song dynasty calligraphy was profoundly influenced by Zen Buddhism, which viewed rules and norms as mere tools, likening them to boats for crossing a river. Once the shore is reached, the boat can be discarded. While ordinary people adhere to rules and norms, the wise transcend them, they thought. Allowing one's heart to guide its desires without crossing boundaries became the ultimate pursuit of Song dynasty calligraphers.

4. Song Ci

The thriving urban life propelled the Song dynasty lyrics, which were sung to music, to new heights. These lyrics, known as "Song ci," were crafted to suit specific musical compositions, featuring varying sentence lengths and rhymes that made them both catchy and captivating. Initially, they predominantly portrayed the romantic attachment between individuals and were widely embraced for entertainment purposes in both the imperial court and among the general populace (fig. 67). During the early Northern Song dynasty, Liu Yong (c. 987–c. 1053), a master of music theory, produced numerous new Song ci works using both existing and novel melodies. His compositions were cherished for their fresh and refined language, vividly depicting scenes of everyday life. Legend has it that wherever there was a well for drinking water, Liu Yong's melodies could be heard echoing in song.

While Liu Yong primarily contributed to the creative techniques of Song ci, Su Shi, in a groundbreaking manner, expanded the thematic scope of the art form, departing from the conventional focus on romantic relationships. He depicted rural life and mountain scenery, engaged in discussions, and

expressed personal feelings, each with its own charm. In addition, Su Shi pioneered a bold and unconstrained style of Song ci, in contrast to the preceding graceful and restrained style, transforming it into a medium for scholars to express their sentiments, significantly enhancing the artistic conception and style of the art form. Song ci embodies the characteristics of the rich life of scholars and the prosperity of secular life, making it a worthy representative of the splendid literary scene of the Song dynasty.

Beyond the Coastline

During the Song dynasty, Zen Buddhist monks pioneered a technique in landscape painting known as "broken ink." In addition to the writing brush, they used dry grass stalks and sugarcane residue to create paintings on paper. By allowing clear water and diluted and concentrated ink to collide on the paper, breaking each other's outlines, they created unique ink variations that portrayed landscapes resembling disappearing clouds and mist. While this painting technique did not thrive in China, it garnered significant attention in Japan, where it is known as haboku. The transmission of this new painting approach to Japan occurred through merchants and monks traveling between China and East Asia, benefiting from the flourishing overseas trade and extensive external exchanges during the Song dynasty

Fig. 67 A mural from a Northern Song dynasty tomb, depicting a musical performance. In the scene, a dancer in the center is gracefully bending forward and raising her sleeves, while musicians on either side play instruments such as the sheng, panpipes, and five-string pipa. The work illustrates how the prosperous commodity economy of the dynasty spurred the development of the entertainment industry, making music and dance an integral part of social life.

in China (fig. 68).

The frequent conflicts between the Song dynasty and the northern nomadic regimes left the commercial land routes to the Western Regions and Central Asia deserted. Consequently, the southeastern maritime routes became the primary channels for external exchanges for Song traders. At the same time, the shifting economic center towards the south provided a strong hinterland for trade with Southeast Asia. Along the coastlines of East and South China, there were not only major ports like Ningbo, Quanzhou, and Guangzhou, but also numerous smaller ports, forming a multi-tiered system. Song dynasty overseas trade primarily targeted Northeast and Southeast Asia, extending as far as South Asia, the Middle East, and the East African coast.

In the waters of Yangjiang, Guangdong Province in South China, a sunken ship named "Nanhai One" was excavated in 2007. The cargo holds of the ship contained well-preserved bundles of ceramics, identified through archaeological examination as export ceramics from local kilns in provinces such as Jiangxi, Zhejiang, and Fujian in southeastern coast of China. Among them were exquisite and luxurious pieces as well as plain and simple ones, indicating a wide range of target consumer groups (fig. 69). It is worth mentioning that over 180 pieces of gold

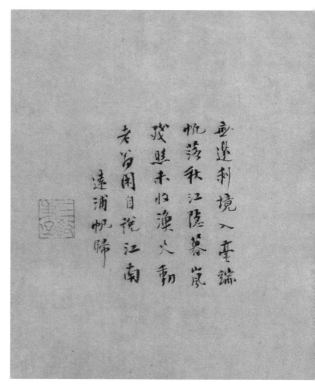

Fig. 68 *Returning Sail on Distant Shores*
Zen Monk Yujian (Southern Song dynasty)
Ink on paper
Length 77 cm, height 30.6 cm
Tokugawa Art Museum, Nagoya

This painting is executed using the broken ink technique, capturing a landscape where clouds and water blend harmoniously, imbued with a Zen-like brushstroke.

Fig. 69 A porcelain bowl from Jingdezhen of Jiangxi Province recovered from the Southern Song dynasty shipwreck, the Nanhai One, in the South China Sea.

Fig. 70 An Arabic-style gold belt found on the shipwreck, the Nanhai One, in the South China Sea.

jewelry were found in the upper cabins of the shipwreck and some items display exotic styles like those from Arabia, suggesting the presence of foreign merchants aboard the ship (fig. 70).

The flourishing market economy of the Song dynasty led to profound changes in the fields of circulation and credit. While the increased activity in commodity trading necessitated more coinage, advancements in production led to greater demand for metals like copper and iron. Meanwhile, the rising economies in neighboring states such as the Liao, Jin, and Western Xia largely relied on the influx of coinage and metals from the Song dynasty, prompting the Song court to tightly control their outflow. These factors combined to create a dearth of coinage in the Song dynasty. To address this, wealthy merchants in southwestern Sichuan devised a form of paper currency known as "jiaozi" during the Northern Song period, which replaced coinage in commercial

transactions (fig. 71). Subsequently, the Song government adopted this innovation, backed by national credit, and issued official jiaozi on a large scale to compensate for the shortage of coinage. During the Southern Song period, the use of paper currency became even more widespread. Although the Song dynasty paper currency eventually collapsed due to over issuance and inflation, the creation of paper currency based on national credit, as well as its use as a fiscal tool in the process of supplementing currency, marked a groundbreaking development in Chinese and world history.

Fig. 71 A rubbing of the jiaozi banknote from the Northern Song dynasty. The vertically long layout is divided into three sections: the upper part features ten symbols of square-holed round coins, the middle part contains neatly arranged text specifying the regions, occasions, and value for which the jiaozi could be used, and the lower part depicts scenes of Song dynasty customs, serving as an anti-counterfeiting mark of the time.

CHAPTER SEVEN
Going Beyond Their Borders: Liao, Western Xia, Jin, and Yuan Dynasties

Even at its zenith, the Song dynasty governed a notably smaller territory in comparison to the Tang dynasty. In the aftermath of the tumultuous late Tang and the era of the Five Dynasties, several non-Han ethnic regimes arose in the vicinity of the Central Plains, traditionally ruled by Han Chinese. Despite the Song rulers' ambitions to reclaim their lost lands, they found themselves obliged to acknowledge the necessity of coexistence with the northern regimes of Liao (916–1125), Western Xia (1038–1227), and Jin (1115–1234), after prolonged conflicts. This division between northern and southern China endured for more than three centuries until it was brought to an end by the Mongols from the northern steppes. Throughout this period, the non-Han ethnic regimes, drawing inspiration from aspects of Song governance, introduced various institutional and cultural reforms to varying degrees, thereby reshaping Chinese political and cultural landscapes by integrating non-Han cultures and traditions into it.

New Elements: the Liao, Western Xia, and Jin

The Liao, Western Xia, and Jin, formidable regimes that long coexisted with the Song, inhabited the steppes and agricultural-pastoral

On the facing page

Fig. 72 Detail of *Departure of the Eastern Dan Prince.* See fig. 73 for the complete painting on pages 120–121.

regions to the north. Embracing a nomadic way of life where livestock products were fundamental for sustenance and attire, these societies contrasted sharply with the agrarian Central Plains, exhibiting distinct economic and social structures. Correspondingly, the independent regimes that emerged in these areas also had different political patterns from those of the Central Plains, with most deliberations taking place in tribal alliances, and power transitions frequently determined by consensus within these alliances or through fraternal succession systems.

I. Rising Liao in the North

The Liao, founded by the Khitan, emerged as the earliest power to challenge the Song dynasty, controlling the northern steppes and the adjacent agricultural-pastoral region of northern China. Legend tells of a meeting at the Liao River between a man riding a white horse from the Laoha River and a woman driving a green ox cart from the Xilamuren River. Their eight sons multiplied, forming the initial eight tribes of the Khitan. This tale suggests the Khitans originated from the amalgamation of the two tribes, each venerating the green ox and the white horse as their totems.

During the onset of the Five Dynasties period following the Tang dynasty's downfall, various powers vied for supremacy in the Central Plains, causing the northern steppes to be overlooked. In 916, Yelü Abaoji (872–926), leader of the Khitan, assumed

▲ **Fig. 73** *Departure of the Eastern Dan Prince*
Li Zanhua (i.e., Yelü Bei, 899–936)
Length 687 cm, height 27.8 cm
Museum of Fine Arts, Boston

Yelü Bei, also known as Li Zanhua, was the eldest son of Yelü Abaoji, known as the Eastern Dan Prince. In this artwork, six figures are depicted riding spirited horses, each with distinct postures and attire reflecting their respective statuses. The Eastern Dan Prince was knowledgeable in music, skilled in medicine, and proficient in both Khitan and Chinese languages, playing a pivotal role in the fusion of Khitan and Han cultures.

◄ **Fig. 74** *Envoys from the Khitan* (detail)
Anonymous (Song dynasty)
Ink and color on silk
Length 252.6 cm, height 33.1 cm (for full scroll)
Palace Museum, Taibei

This is a section of a long scroll depicting scenes from the negotiations between the Song and Liao dynasties.

control of the northern tribal coalition and founded the Liao dynasty, predating the Song dynasty, which was patterned after Han-style governance. Declaring himself emperor, Yelü Abaoji (Emperor Taizu of Liao) sought to expand his dominion southward into the Central Plains. His ambition was realized by his son, Emperor Taizong, Yelü Deguang (reigned 927–947), who seized the opportunity presented by Later Tang's (one of the Five Dynasties in the north) internal turmoil, capturing control of the sixteen prefectures of Youyun (encompassing present-day Beijing and the northern regions

of Tianjin, Hebei and Shanxi provinces), thereby confronting the Han Chinese dynasty. Yelü Abaoji chose to depart from the Khitan tradition of fraternal succession, adopting the Han hereditary system where the eldest son inherited the throne. However, the subsequent imperial succession process was full of turbulence, impacting its southern expansion efforts (fig. 73).

Following the unification of China, the Song dynasty sought to reclaim the lost territory of the sixteen prefectures from the Liao, who, in turn, sought to expand southward and exert control over the Song. The marshland region of central Hebei (now a province in North China) acted as a natural barrier against the steppe cavalry, where Song and Liao forces engaged in a protracted struggle, marked by victories and setbacks on both sides, ultimately resulting in a stalemate. In 1005, after significant battles where both rulers personally led campaigns, the Song and Liao dynasties concluded the Chanyuan Treaty, mutually recognizing each other's sovereignty and agreeing to maintain their respective borders (fig. 74). Under the terms, the Song pledged to pay the Liao 100,000 taels of silver and 200,000 bolts of silk annually. These agreements reflected an approximate balance of power, with the Liao holding a slight advantage.

Over 30 years later, during the second year of the Qingli reign (1042) of Emperor Renzong, seizing upon the Song dynasty's conflicts with the Western Xia, the Liao compelled the Song to significantly increase the annual payments, this time as tributes paid by a vassal state, an event known as the "Qingli Tribute Increase." Faced with the dilemma of escalating costs of war with the Liao and the tributes demanded, the weaker Song dynasty opted for compromise, leading to a peaceful period between the two that lasted for over a century.

The Liao dynasty emperors maintained their traditional nomadic and hunting lifestyle, with distinct palaces designated for each season, which were known as "seasonal nabos," with nabo being a Khitan term for "camp." During each season, the imperial family engaged in specific activities: catching geese and fishing in spring, falconry in summer, deer hunting in autumn, and tiger hunting in winter. The wall paintings at Qingling, a Liao tomb, vividly depict these imperial activities across different seasons (fig. 75). While the nabos primarily consisted of felt tents typical of northern nomadic life, the Liao emperors and empresses resided in permanent Han-style palaces, often accompanied by an ancestral temple dedicated to the emperor's ancestors.

Additionally, the Liao dynasty constructed five capital cities, which served as expansive military fortresses to exert control over various regions. However, the Liao emperors preferred to conduct state affairs in the nabo palaces. During their seasonal migrations, the emperor was accompanied by numerous imperial relatives and high-ranking officials. Military and political assemblies were convened in the nabo palaces, solidifying them as the true political hubs of the Liao dynasty.

The Khitan originally lacked a writing system. However, after the establishment of the new dynasty, Yelü Abaoji initiated the development of two writing systems in order to meet the needs of development and communication: the large script and the small script. The Khitan large script was directly derived from the Chinese writing system, but with fewer characters and fewer strokes per character. It adopted or adapted Chinese character sounds, shapes, and meanings to pronounce Khitan words (fig. 76). The small script, on the other hand, was a simplified version of the large script, comprising approximately 400 basic characters. While the small script retained some resemblance to Chinese characters, it evolved into a phonetic writing system specifically for spelling the Khitan language, which belongs to the Tungusic language family.

The Liao court etiquette was also characterized by the fusion of the northern

Fig. 75 In the mural *Four Seasons Landscape* from the Qingling Tomb of Emperor Shengzong of Liao, the "Spring Water" section depicts a focal point on hunting geese during the spring season.

Fig. 76 A rubbing of the Khitan large script from stele inscription.

Fig. 77　The ruins of the Western Xia Heishui City in Ejina Banner, Inner Mongolia Autonomous Region.

nomadic traditions with Han traditions. For instance, on New Year's Day, officials paid homage to the emperor at court, following a Han custom. Concurrently, Khitan customs like the shaman's New Year's Eve fire worship were observed.

Despite governing vast territories spanning both nomadic and agrarian regions, the Liao dynasty had already undergone significant assimilation into Han administrative practices.

2. Western Xia in the Northwest

The Liao and Song dynasties were entrenched in a prolonged standoff, yet this balance was disrupted during the reigns of Emperors Renzong of Song (reigned 1022–1063) and Xingzong of Liao (reigned 1031–1055) by the rise of the Western Xia. The founders of the Western Xia were the Tanguts, originating from the Qiang ethnic group and initially residing in the borderlands of Sichuan, Qinghai, and Gansu provinces. As the Tang dynasty approached its end, pressured by the Tibetan regime, they migrated westward to northern Shaanxi through

western Gansu. By the dynasty's collapse, the Tangut Tuoba clan, amid the suppression of the peasant uprising led by Huang Chao, had transformed into a provincial military commission known as the Xiazhou Dingnan Army, adopting the surname Li from the Tang emperor. During the Five Dynasties period, though ostensibly swearing allegiance to the Han dynasties, they operated as a de facto semi-independent local authority. Upon the establishment of the Song dynasty, the Tanguts sought to maintain their original semi-independent status, conflicting with the Song court's centralization policy, leading to mutual hostility. While the Tanguts raided the northwest borderlands of the Song, the Song undertook military siege, economic blockade and other ways to counteract. In 1038, during Emperor Renzong of Song's reign, Li Yuanhao (1003–1048), a Tangut leader with a strong sense of nationalism, established the state of Daxia, later known as the Western Xia, and declared himself emperor. Controlling the Hexi Corridor in the northwest, the Western Xia emerged as a significant adversary to the Song (fig. 77).

The emergence of the Western Xia introduced uncertainty into the ongoing confrontation between the Song and the Liao, disrupting their equilibrium. Initially, the Western Xia formed an alliance with the Liao against the Song. Li Yuanhao, the ruler of the Western Xia, established martial bonds with the Liao court and offered spoils acquired from wars against the Song to the Liao in exchange for their support. Taking advantage of the situation, the Liao demanded increased annual tributes from the Song. Upon the Song's compliance, they pressured the Western Xia to cease hostilities with the Song, inciting dissatisfaction from the Western Xia. The dynamics among the three regimes fluctuated, characterized by sporadic warfare and alliances, shaping a triangular power balance.

After the Jin emerged victorious over the Liao, the Western Xia sought to become a vassal state to the Jin as a gesture of goodwill. Following the Jin's defeat of the Northern Song, which prompted the Song dynasty to relocate its capital to Hangzhou in southern China, the Western Xia found itself no longer sharing a border with the Song dynasty. Instead, it primarily engaged in interactions with the Jin, maintaining over 80 years of friendly trade relations. However, the greatest threat to the Western Xia came from the Mongols. During Genghis Khan's campaigns against other Mongolian tribes, the Western Xia had sheltered enemies of Genghis Khan, resulting in multiple Mongol invasions. When the Western Xia sought assistance from the Jin court, they were rebuffed, leading to hostility between the two sides. After more than 10 years of warfare, both sides suffered heavy losses and were subsequently conquered by the Mongols.

At the establishment of the Western Xia state, a robust ethnic identity was prevalent. Before Li Yuanhao declared himself emperor, he announced the abandonment of surnames bestowed by the Tang and Song dynasties.

Fig. 78 The hairstyle of Tangut men is clearly evident in the murals of the Western Xia period (1038–1227) discovered in the Yulin Grottoes of Gansu Province. The Yulin Grottoes share similar artistic content and style with the Mogao Grottoes, representing a branch of the Mogao Grottoes art system.

Upon ascending the throne, he promptly issued the "baldness edict," mandating strict adherence to the Tangut hairstyle— shaving the crown of the head while leaving hair on the sides (fig. 78). Li Yuanhao also commissioned the scholar Yeli Renrong to devise the Tangut script and promoted its use. Consequently, not only all official documents but most Buddhist scriptures, literary works, and everyday writings were written in this script. Today, The *Pearl in the Palm*, a bilingual glossary between the Chinese and Tangut languages, completed in 1190 by the Tangut scholar Gule Maocai, serves as a crucial tool for deciphering texts in the Western Xia script.

Although Li Yuanhao harbored a strong

Fig. 79 The Western Xia Buddhist murals in the Yulin Grottoes, which exhibit the stylistic characteristics of Song dynasty landscape painting, represent one of the manifestations of cultural integration among various ethnic groups during the period.

3. Jin in the Northeast

The Jin dynasty, rising to prominence north of the Liao, was established by the semi-nomadic Jurchens. They inhabited the basins of the Heilong River and the Songhua River, adopting a semi-settled and rough agricultural lifestyle that blended farming and hunting. After defeating both the Liao and Northern Song dynasties, the Jin dynasty engaged in a prolonged conflict with the Southern Song.

During Emperor Huizong of Song's reign (1100–1126), pearl jewelry surged in popularity among the nobility of the Song dynasty. At that time, most of the pearls of the Song dynasty were purchased from the Liao through the markets on the Song-Liao border, and the Liao's pearls were harvested in regions inhabited by the Jurchens. Local inhabitants collected pearls with a very special method. There was a kind of swan that retained the pearls in their crops after consuming the flesh of freshwater pearl mussels. A specialized sea eagle was trained for swan hunting. So people caught swans with this sea eagle (fig. 80),

ethnic identity, he structured an administrative system mirroring that of the Song dynasty. Beginning in 1061, he also decided to discontinue the use of Tangut national etiquette in court activities, and to switch completely to Han-style etiquette. While top-level and some official positions were exclusively reserved for Tangut individuals, others were accessible to both Tangut and Han candidates. This arrangement, while upholding the dominance of Tangut nobility, offered promising career paths for the Han Chinese. Positioned in the Hexi Corridor, a hub of ethnic mingling, the Western Xia, despite its emphasis on Tangut identity, evolved into a culturally diverse regime (fig. 79).

Fig. 80 A Sea Eagle Hunting a Swan
Jin dynasty (1115–1234)
Diameter 7 cm, thickness 2.1 cm
The Palace Museum, Beijing

This jade ornament is carved with the scene of a sea eagle catching a swan. There is a hole on each side of the ornament, likely used for threading a belt or attaching it to a hook, indicating it was a type of clothing accessory.

and then collected expensive pearls from the swan's crop. However, this industry ultimately spelled disaster for the Liao dynasty. In their quest for more pearls to trade with the Song, the Khitans frequently demanded additional sea eagles from the Jurchens while imposing hefty demands of ginseng, horses, pearls, and sable fur, creating a heavy burden for the Jurchen.

In 1114, Wanyan Aguda (1068–1123), leader of the Jurchen, rebelled against the Liao dynasty and proclaimed himself emperor the following year, establishing the Jin dynasty. Learning of Jin's rise, the Song dynasty established contact with the Jin via maritime routes from the Shandong Peninsula to northeastern Liao in the name of buying horses. In 1120, the two powers signed an

alliance treaty, strategizing a joint offensive against the Liao dynasty. It was agreed that after defeating the Liao, the Great Wall would serve as their mutual boundary, and the tributes the Song had been paying to the Liao would be redirected to the Jin.

However, the joint military campaign between the Song and Jin exposed the Song army's inadequacies. In 1127, two years after the Jin toppled the Liao, they launched an assault on the Northern Song dynasty, compelling it to relocate its capital southward. Following two rounds of negotiations, the Song submitted to the Jin, agreeing to pay an annual tribute of 250,000 taels of silver and 250,000 pieces of silk. At the same time, the boundary between the two dynasties shifted southward to the middle reaches of the Huai

directly reporting to him upon his accession: the Central Secretariat, the Chancellery, and the Department of State Affairs. Subsequently, Wanyan Liang (reigned 1149–1161), who seized power through a coup, enacted further administrative reforms to consolidate his imperial authority. Among these reforms was the crucial decision to relocate the capital to Beijing, symbolizing the shift of the political center of the Jin dynasty southward to the agricultural heartland.

Simultaneously, the mass migration of Jurchen people to North China catalyzed rapid agricultural progress. Southern Song emissaries visiting the Jin were struck by the fertile lands and abundant harvests of North China under Jin rule. The renowned Lugou Bridge (figs. 81–82), also recognized as the Marco Polo Bridge, spanning the Yongding River in the western outskirts of Beijing, was erected during the Jin dynasty, serving

Fig. 81 (above) and fig. 82 (right) The Lugou Bridge in Fengtai district, Beijing, was originally built during the Jin dynasty. Spanning the Yongding River, it is the oldest existing stone arch bridge in Beijing. Each railing of the bridge is topped with a carved stone lion (enlarged on the right).

River, extending to the Dasanguan Pass (present-day northern foothills of the Qin Mountains, Baoji, Shaanxi Province).

As the Jin dynasty asserted control over the Central Plains agricultural region, historically the heartland of Han Chinese dynasties, significant shifts occurred in its political landscape. Emperor Xizong of Jin (reigned 1135–1149), inspired by the bureaucratic frameworks of the Tang and Song dynasties, instituted three key departments as a testament to the flourishing commerce and travel of that period. As Jurchen migrants assimilated into the agrarian traditions of the Han Chinese, they swiftly embraced Han customs, language, and dress. Embracing the scholarly culture of the Han Chinese literati, the affluent Jurchen aristocracy developed a profound interest in Han literature and history, actively engaging in poetic exchanges and immersing themselves in Han poetry.

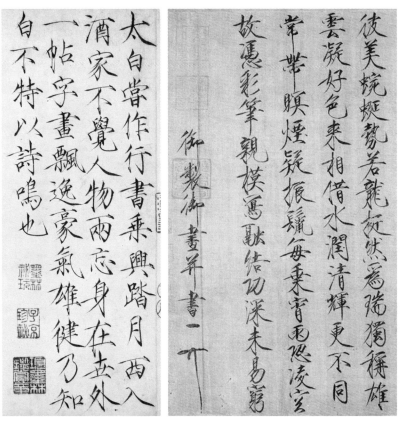

Figs. 83–84 Calligraphic works by Emperor Zhangzong of Jin (left) and Emperor Huizong of Song (right).

The Jin rulers were deeply concerned about the loss of their ethnic traditions, especially the martial spirit, due to the rapid Sinicization of the Jurchen. Emperors Shizong (reigned 1161–1189) and Zhangzong (reigned 1190–1208) of Jin sought to counter the process by promoting the learning and use of the Jurchen script, making it mandatory for the imperial examinations. They also personally engaged in activities to enhance equestrian archery training. However, the process of Sinicization among the Jurchen people continued unabated. Emperor Zhangzong himself excelled in Han poetry, calligraphy, and painting, resembling literati of the Han ethnicity. He adopted the "slender gold script" modeled after Emperor Huizong of the Song dynasty, embodying both form and spirit (figs. 83–84).

Meanwhile, the Mongols, another martial ethnic group, emerged on the northern steppes. As the political center shifted southward, the Jin dynasty, following the example of the Han Chinese, constructed an extensive border defense system known as the "boundary ditch," consisting of walls, moats, and fortresses along the northern frontier. However, this defensive barrier proved ineffective against the military prowess of the Mongols. Pressured by Mongol advances, the Jin court retreated to Kaifeng and eventually succumbed to Mongol conquest in 1234.

The Liao, Western Xia, and Jin dynasties all rose in the northern steppes and the transitional zone between agriculture and pastoralism, thriving with both nomadic and agrarian economies. Their governmental structures continuously integrated tribal political customs with the centralized Han Chinese system. This amalgamation of new elements into the dynastic framework from the Han to Tang periods significantly enhanced the inclusiveness of diverse economies and cultures.

Conquerors on Horseback: The Yuan

After the decline of the Tang dynasty, multiple tribes contended for supremacy across the northern steppes. Among them, the Khitan and Jin emerged as dominant forces, instituting centralized governance systems inspired by those of the Han dynasties. Nonetheless, their authority over the majority of tribes remained limited. Temüjin (1162–1227) of the Mongol tribe, renowned for his strategic acumen in warfare, rose to prominence amidst this competition, eventually uniting the disparate tribes. In the spring of 1206, Temüjin established the Yeke Mongghul Ulus (Mongol Empire) and assumed the title of Genghis Khan (fig. 85). Under his leadership, the various tribes of the steppes coalesced into a unified entity, collectively known as the Mongols.

1. Going Beyond the Steppes

Throughout Chinese history, steppe regimes had essentially been tribal alliances led by conquerors over blood-related tribal communities. The Mongol Empire, established by Genghis Khan through military conquest, was no exception in its early days. However, he dismantled the relative independence and integrity of the subdued tribes by introducing the mingghan, a system of social structure based on a social-military unit of 1000 households (fig. 86). This system mixed members of various tribes, combining military and civilian administration, thus mitigating the loose structure of tribal alliances and integrating the steppe tribes into a unified Mongolian ethnicity. The system was also intended

Fig. 85 A portrait of Genghis Khan (Temüjin) housed in the National Museum of China, Beijing.

Fig. 86 The bronze seal used by a Yuan dynasty military official titled "Baihu," which denotes a senior rank. This is housed in Changsha Museum, Hunan Province.

to ensure the disappearance of old tribal identities, replacing them with loyalty to the Mongol Empire. Additionally, Genghis Khan selected a group of nobles and elite warriors to form the Kheshig, the Khan's personal guard, directly commanded by the Khan's confidants. This not only strengthened the Khan's personal authority but also facilitated his direct control over certain nobles. It can be said that Genghis Khan established a unique form of centralized power on the steppe.

While the war to unify the tribes of the steppes was ongoing, Genghis Khan initiated military campaigns beyond their borders. Following the establishment of the Mongol Empire, expansion became the primary objective for Genghis Khan and his successors. The empire launched three massive campaigns to the west, sweeping through Khwarezmia Empire (fig. 87) and the Abbasid Caliphate Empire, stretching its influence into Central Asia, West Asia, and even Eastern Europe, fundamentally reshaping the political map of Eurasia. In the south, the Mongols defeated the Western Xia in 1227 and the Jin in 1234. By 1252, Mongol forces marched southward along the Liupan Mountains (the present-day junction of Ningxia, Gansu, and Shaanxi provinces), subjugating the southwestern regions of Tibet and Dali, and encircling the Southern Song dynasty. Ultimately, in 1279, they conquered the Southern Song dynasty.

2. The Establishment of the Yuan Dynasty

In 1260, Kublai Khan (fig. 88) assumed the throne, becoming the fifth Great Khan of the

Fig. 88 It shows Kublai Khan, Emperor Shizu of the Yuan dynasty wearing a silver leather warming cap and white robes, depicting his elderly countenance. This portrait is housed in the Palace Museum, Taibei.

Mongol Empire. Recognizing the military prowess of his predecessors but noting their governance deficiencies, he initiated reforms modeled after the Han dynasties, departing from their traditional nomadic-centric policies. Through an enthronement edict composed in refined Chinese, he conveyed to the people of the Han region that he not only held the title of Khan of the Mongols but also claimed the position of Emperor of a new dynasty in China. In 1271, drawing inspiration from the Han classic *Yijing* (also known as *Book of Changes*), he named his dynasty the "Great Yuan." The subsequent year saw the official establishment of the Yuan dynasty's (1271–1368) capital in Yanjing (present-day Beijing), renamed Dadu, marking the transition of the ruling center from the steppes to the agricultural heartland. Known as "Khanbaliq" to

On the facing page

Fig. 87 A painting contained in the 13th-century manuscript *The History of the World Conqueror* by the Persian historian the Persian Ata-Malik Juvayni (1226–1283), depicting the scene of Genghis Khan's army attacking Khwarazm. This is housed in the British Museum in London.

Fig. 89 A panoramic model of Beijing city, where the central axis running through the Imperial Palace is clearly evident. This central axis was first established during the Yuan dynasty.

Fig. 90 Zhuanta Hutong, originally built in the Yuan dynasty, located in Xicheng District, Beijing.

Central Asian Turkic speakers, Dadu was meticulously planned, featuring a north-south axis (fig. 89) which continues to play a guiding role today lined with evenly arranged east-west lanes called "hutongs." The term "hutong" is derived from the Mongolian word "huddug," meaning "well." Today, many streets in Beijing still bear the name "hutong" (fig. 90).

As early as 1259, prior to the establishment of the Yuan dynasty, Kublai Khan oversaw the construction of a city in what is now the Plain Blue Banner, Inner Mongolia in North China. Blending elements of traditional Han city planning with considerations for Mongolian nomadic life, the city eventually became known as "Shangdu" (Upper Capital). Following the Yuan dynasty's relocation of its capital to Dadu, Shangdu served as the summer capital. Yuan emperors typically resided in Dadu during the autumn and winter seasons, and in Shangdu during the spring and summer seasons. Many significant political events of the Yuan dynasty unfolded during the emperors' travels between these two capitals, effectively continuing the Liao dynasty's "seasonal nabo" system.

During Kublai Khan's reign (1260–1294), his Han Confucian advisors played a significant role in shaping a bureaucratic system that mirrored that of the Han dynasties. The central government was organized into the Central Secretariat, responsible for administration; the Council of Military Affairs, overseeing military affairs; and the Censorate, tasked with surveillance. The Central Secretariat was further divided into six ministries—Personnel, Revenue, Rites, War, Justice, and Works—each handling specific administrative functions. At the local level, Branch Secretariats were established to supervise regions, prefectures, districts, and counties. This bureaucratic framework served

to curb the privileges of Mongol nobles and consolidate central authority.

In addition to administrative reforms, Kublai Khan prioritized agriculture, establishing a dedicated institution within the central government to compile the *Fundamentals of Agriculture and Sericulture*, aimed at guiding agricultural practices (fig. 91). Confucianism, previously overlooked by the Mongols, gained recognition during Kublai Khan's reign. Consequently, the Mongol-led Yuan dynasty had become fully Sinicized. The conflicts between the Yuan and the Southern Song thus evolved into struggles for annexation and unification between the two Han Chinese regimes.

During the Yuan dynasty's campaign to

Fig. 91 *Rice Culture*
Yuan dynasty
Metropolitan Museum of Art, New York

It depicts China's most fundamental economic activity in the south: the cultivation and harvesting of rice.

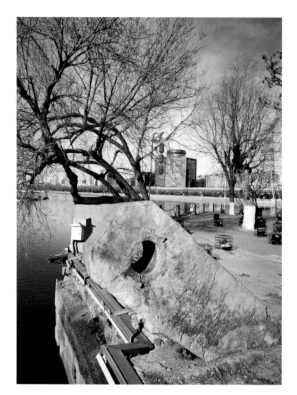

Fig. 92 Pingjin Lock, the only remaining Yuan dynasty ship lock site on the Grand Canal, is now seen in Chaoyang District, Beijing.

Hubs Connecting the World

The Liao, Western Xia, and Jin dynasties dominated northern China, often in conflict with the Song dynasty. Despite frequent armed conflicts, there were significant economic exchanges between the northern and southern regions, both officially and among civilians. Unlike agrarian economies, the nomadic economies of the northern ethnic regimes were less self-sufficient and stable, leading to trade becoming a crucial means of supplementing resources. The Song dynasty, especially the Southern Song, took advantage of the sea to temporarily avoid nomadic harassment and engaged in extensive maritime trade with East Asian and Southeast Asian countries. Consequently, despite the north-south division during this period, these regimes maintained and expanded their connections with the wider world.

1. Trading Routes and Systems

The Shangjing (Upper Capital), one of the five capitals of the Liao dynasty, situated in the present-day town of Lindong, Balin Left Banner, Chifeng, Inner Mongolia, served not only as a military stronghold but also as a bustling commercial hub. The western section of Shangjing was home to craftsmen and merchants, many of whom hailed from Shanxi, Hebei, and other neighboring regions. Near the southern gate, a camp was set up for the Uighur traders crossing the steppes. Nanjing (Southern Capital), present-day Beijing, stood out as the most vibrant among the five capitals. A bustling market thrived in the city's north, facilitating the trade of various goods from both land and sea. The silver and silk acquired by the Liao from the Song through the Chanyuan Treaty and the Qingli Tribute Increase were utilized as currency and traded as commodities in exchanges with merchants from Northeast Asia, Central Asia, and beyond. The

unify China, the southern region endured significantly less devastation in the wars compared to the north. With the government prioritizing agriculture more than ever, agricultural activities in the south swiftly rebounded after the conflicts ceased. This pattern mirrors the historical trend of China's economic center shifting southward since the Sui and Tang dynasties. While the political capital remained in the north, the economic focus gradually shifted to the south, highlighting the necessity of fortifying economic bonds between the two regions.

The Grand Canal, originally constructed during the Sui dynasty, passed through Luoyang in the middle before bending westward. However, the Yuan dynasty altered the canal's course, rerouting it from Beijing through Shandong and Jiangsu directly to Hangzhou, bypassing Luoyang, so its whole course was almost straight. This reconfiguration laid the groundwork for the contemporary layout of the Grand Canal in China (fig. 92).

Fig. 93 Aerial view of the Hexi Corridor.

transliteration "Khitan" was widely spread through trade and became synonymous with "China" in Persian, Western Turkic languages, and East Slavic languages, a legacy that endures to this day.

Nestled along the Hexi Corridor (fig. 93), the historic trade artery since the Han and Tang dynasties, the Western Xia held sway over vital transport routes linking the Central Plains to the Western Regions, as well as facilitating trade between the Mongolian steppes and the expansive territories of Gansu, Qinghai, and Tibet. Through the Western Xia, coveted goods like silk, porcelain, and lacquerware from the Central Plains found their way to the Western Regions, while spices and livestock journeyed back to the heartland. Following conflicts with the Song dynasty, the Western Xia, emulating the practices of the Liao dynasty, levied substantial tributes

of silver, silk, and tea from the Song dynasty, which they then traded with other nations. This tradition was later embraced by the Jin dynasty, which succeeded the Liao.

As trade partners of the Liao, Western Xia, and Jin dynasties primarily occupied positions within the Eurasian continent, the Song dynasty, boasting an extensive coastline along the eastern edge of Eurasia, assumed a pivotal role as a transit hub for both overland and maritime commerce. Sailing vessels laden with commodities such as porcelain departed from Song ports of Guangzhou, Quanzhou, and Ningbo, bound for markets in the Indochina Peninsula and other places of Southeast Asia. And these maritime routes extended furthest into the Indian Ocean to the shores of East Africa, circumnavigating the southern tip of the Malay Peninsula. Upon their return

Fig. 94 Details of an illustration showing "Marco Polo Traveling in a Caravan," a fourteenth-century painting housed in the Bibliothèque Nationale in Paris, France.

from Southeast Asia, ships brought back cargoes of spices and other goods, meeting the demands of the Song populace while also supplying regions including the Liao, Western Xia, Jin, and even deeper into the Eurasian continent.

Furthermore, the Song dynasty maintained maritime ties with Goryeo (Korea) and Japan. Notably, Goryeo served as a vital conduit for the Song to procure horses from the northeast, circumventing areas under the dominion of the Liao and Jin dynasties.

After the rise of the Mongol Empire, the Mongols kept a small portion of its agricultural tax revenue for administrative purposes, entrusting the majority to joint venture trading organizations known as "ortoq" to expand commerce across Eurasia. These ortoqs, primarily consisting of Uyghurs and Muslims, were skilled in

lending operations. It is highly likely that the Venetian Polo family, including Marco Polo (fig. 94), his father, and uncle, who conducted business in China during Kublai Khan's reign, were among the Mongol Empire's ortoqs.

When the Yuan dynasty unified China's north and south, the extensive territories in Central Asia, West Asia, and Europe under the control of the Mongol Empire fragmented into four major khanates: the Ilkhanate, the Chagatai Khanate, the Golden Horde, and the House of Ögedei. The relay station system of the Yuan dynasty also extended into the territories of these four khanates. Along these routes, travelers could journey from Dadu westward to the capital of the Golden Horde, Sarai (situated north of present-day Astrakhan, Russia) on the banks of the Volga River. Moving southwestward, they could reach the capital of the Ilkhanate, Tabriz, in northwestern present-day Iran, via present-day Yunnan Province in Southwest China. The people of the Yuan dynasty proudly proclaimed, "Traveling ten thousand miles is like strolling in one's own courtyard."

During the mid-13th to mid-14th centuries, known as the "Pax Mongolica" (Latin for "Mongol peace") era, the trade networks from East Asia to Western Europe, which previously necessitated multiple intermediaries and numerous checkpoints for connectivity, experienced unprecedented ease and openness (fig. 95). The Silk Road, which had declined since the mid-Tang dynasty, flourished once again. The Yuan dynasty established trade connections with Europe through the Golden Horde and forged links with Arabia and Anatolia through the Ilkhanate.

Fig. 96 The twin pagodas in Kaiyuan Temple in Quanzhou, Fujian Province. On the upper left of the picture are the flowers of Citong tree.

The Yuan dynasty inherited the thriving maritime trade of the Song dynasty. Three major southern seaports—Guangzhou, Quanzhou (see fig. 97 on page 138), and Ningbo—hosted specialized overseas trade offices. Among them, Quanzhou, also known as "Zayton" in Arabic and English, meaning the "City of Citong/Erythrina Tree," stood out as the largest due to the Erythrina trees lining its streets (fig. 96). Diverse overseas cultures found their way into China through both maritime and overland trade routes. For example, Islamic artifacts in Quanzhou mainly bore Arabic inscriptions, while those in Dadu predominantly featured Persian inscriptions. This divergence can be attributed to Arabs primarily traveling from the Persian Gulf to southern China via sea routes, while most Central Asians entering northern China through overland routes hailed from Persian-speaking regions or Turkic-speaking areas where Persian was used for religious purposes.

The Grand Canal played a pivotal role in connecting maritime trade routes in East Asia with overland trade routes in Inner Asia in Yuan dynasty territory. Dadu (Beijing) and Hangzhou emerged as the economic hubs of the north and south, respectively, serving as the northern and southern endpoints of the canal. Along the canal's route, numerous burgeoning industrial and commercial towns flourished, including Huai'an in Jiangsu Province, Linqing and Jining in Shandong Province.

Fig. 95 A Yuan dynasty "express courier" pottery figurine carrying a parcel, illustrating the image of couriers rushing along the roads at that time.

2. Two-Way Communication with the Outside World

The most well-known account of the bustling scenes along the Grand Canal during the Yuan dynasty is commonly credited to *The Travels of Marco Polo*, based on oral narratives of Marco Polo (1254–1324), a Venetian merchant who traveled across Asia from 1271 to 1295 and spent 17 years in China. This classic of travel literature presented a captivating image of China to Europe, profoundly influencing European perceptions of the prosperous East. Polo, however, was not the first Westerner to venture into the vast Chinese territories. An early explorer was Franciscan friar John of Plano Carpini (Giovanni da Pian del Carpini, c. 1185–1252), who, in 1246, journeyed on behalf of Pope Innocent IV to the imperial capital of Karakorum after a challenging overland trek. Similarly, William of Rubruck (Willem van Ruysbroeck, c. 1215–c. 1295), a Flemish friar, undertook a mission to Karakorum (near the Erdene Zuu Monastery

Fig. 97 The Liusheng Pagoda, originally serving as a lighthouse at Quanzhou Port during the Song and Yuan dynasties, is located in present-day Shishi, Fujian Province. It was also the first lighthouse along the Maritime Silk Road, witnessing the thriving maritime trade of that era.

in today's Övörkhangai Province, Mongolia) in 1253 as an emissary of Louis IX, King of France. In 1294, John of Montecorvino (Giovanni da Montecorvino, 1247–1328), an Italian Franciscan missionary dispatched by Pope Nicholas IV, arrived in China via sea route and presented the pope's letters to Emperor Chengzong of Yuan (reigned 1294–1307) in Dadu. Later, Odoric of Pordenone (c. 1280–1331), another Franciscan friar, journeyed from Venice by sea to China, where he met Montecorvino in Dadu.

Nestorian Christianity, once introduced during the Tang dynasty but later vanished, experienced a revival during the Yuan dynasty. Kublai Khan's mother was a Nestorian Christian, though she also practiced Buddhism and Taoism. The

Fig. 98 The Kenchō-ji Temple, founded by Song and Yuan dynasty Zen monks, is located in Kamakura City, Japan.

Mongols embraced various religions, even considering Confucianism as a religious belief.

Chinese travelers also ventured to Europe, Africa, and other Asian nations. Rabban Bar Sauma, a Uighur born in Dadu who practiced Nestorian Christianity, journeyed to Europe, where he met with King Philip IV of France, King Edward I of England, and Pope Nicholas IV, receiving warm hospitality. In 1336, Emperor Shundi of Yuan (reigned 1333–1368) dispatched a 16-member delegation to the Roman Curia to meet Pope Benedict XII in Avignon, in southern France. During the reign of Emperor Chengzong, the Yuan court sent envoys to places like Somalia and Morocco in Africa to procure rare animals such as lions and leopards. The Yuan dynasty navigator Wang Dayuan (b. 1311) sailed multiple times from Quanzhou aboard merchant ships to dozens of countries in South Asia and East Africa. His book, *A Brief Account of Island Barbarians*, documented the landscapes and customs he encountered along the way.

During Kublai Khan's rule, the Yuan dynasty waged two unsuccessful wars against Japan, resulting in a lack of official relations between the two nations. Nevertheless, the trade between them persisted, with Ningbo emerging as a pivotal trading port. Japanese Buddhist monks embarked on voyages to China aboard merchant vessels to exchange Buddhist doctrines, with their numbers exceeding those of the Tang and Song eras. Chinese Zen monks often accepted invitations from their Japanese counterparts or the Kamakura shogunate, journeying eastward to propagate the Dharma or oversee Zen temples. They were known in Japan as "visiting monks." Concurrently, amidst the "Pax Mongolica" across Eurasia, Japan experienced what is termed the "Century of Visiting Monks" (fig. 98).

CHAPTER EIGHT
Epochal Changes in Chinese History:
Ming and Qing Dynasties

From the end of the Song dynasty onward, various non-Han cultural traditions were integrated into Chinese culture due to the rule of the Liao, Jin, and Western Xia. This cultural convergence was further strengthened during reunification under the Yuan dynasty and reached new heights during the Ming and Qing dynasties. Through the fusion of various ethnic groups, the vast territory of contemporary China as a unified multi-ethnic state and the strong sense of shared identity of the Chinese nation were established.

Continuing the trend that had been occurring since the Song dynasty, imperial power strengthened during the Ming and Qing dynasties. The vibrant scholar-officials of the Song dynasty, marginalized under imperial pressure, found active roles in rural areas. During the Ming and Qing dynasties, they resurfaced as local gentry. Meanwhile, the flourishing commercial economy integrated the identity of merchants into the local gentry class. The literati and merchants, as part of the local gentry, formed the backbone of maintaining order in grassroots society and nurtured the forces of innovation in modern China.

On the facing page

Fig. 99 Aerial view of the Ming dynasty Imperial Palace ruins located in present-day Nanjing, Jiangsu Province, known as the Ancient Capital of Six Dynasties.

Emperors and Local Gentry

The Yuan dynasty possessed vast territories spanning multiple ecological zones, serving as a hub for interactions between the heartland of the Eurasian continent and the East Asian seas. Although it inherited the governance frameworks of previous dynasties, including the Song, Liao, Western Xia, and Jin, the Yuan still faced challenges in managing a nation with diverse ecological zones and multi-ethnic groups. Consequently, peasant uprisings erupted in the middle and lower reaches of the Yellow and Yangtze Rivers.

I. The Pinnacle of Imperial Power

During the peasant uprisings at the end of the Yuan dynasty, Zhu Yuanzhang (1328–1398) rose to prominence. Born into a poor peasant family, he lost his parents at a young age and was forced to become a monk, begging for alms to survive. In the midst of the chaos, Zhu Yuanzhang stood out. He later joined the rebel army and achieved numerous military successes. Rising from beggar to emperor, he established the Ming dynasty in 1368, setting the capital in Nanjing, and subsequently marched north to overthrow the Yuan dynasty (fig. 99).

Attributing the fall of the Yuan dynasty to the excessive power held by imperial prime ministers, Zhu Yuanzhang assumed absolute power as emperor, appointing only a few Grand Secretaries as advisors. The process of

Fig. 100 The Changling Tomb of Zhu Di, Emperor Chengzu of the Ming dynasty, located in Changping District, Beijing, is the joint burial site of Zhu Di (commonly known as Yongle Emperor) and his empress. Covering an area of approximately 120,000 square meters, it was inscribed on the UNESCO World Heritage List in 2003.

Fig. 101 A portrait of Nurhaci housed in the Palace Museum, Beijing.

consolidating imperial authority was marked by purges of his founding officials. Zhu Yuanzhang trusted his descendants more than these officials to protect the imperial family, but this arrangement led to significant upheaval in the early years of his dynasty after his death.

After Zhu Yuanzhang's death, his grandson Zhu Yunwen (1377–1402?) ascended to the throne and sought to weaken the power of the princes to prevent them from threatening imperial authority. However, Zhu Yuanzhang's fourth son, Prince of Yan, Zhu Di (reigned 1402–1424), who was responsible for defending the northern borders with a large military force, responded preemptively by launching a rebellion. Ultimately, Zhu Di seized the throne from his nephew and moved the capital to Beijing (fig. 100). Having gained the throne through rebellion, Zhu Di was acutely aware of the dangers posed by powerful princes and, upon his ascension, stripped them of their military power.

Fig. 102 Located in Qinhuangdao, Hebei Province, Shanhai Pass is renowned as the "First Pass under Heaven."

Additionally, Zhu Di expanded on the Grand Secretariat system established by his father, Zhu Yuanzhang, forming an inner cabinet as the highest decision-making body to assist him. To prevent officials from plotting against him, he established an institution, primarily led by eunuchs, to oversee and monitor officials, operating above the judicial system. Zhu Di's measures to strengthen imperial power profoundly influenced the political landscape of the Ming dynasty.

Zhu Di moved the capital north to Beijing partly because it had long been his power base and partly because, in his view, his dynasty, as the successor to the Yuan, should control the northern steppes. In this vision, Beijing was the center of his realm. Although the Ming dynasty's northern expansion eventually halted at the Great Wall, it established formal administrative control over the present-day Northeast China. Local specialties such as ginseng and sable fur were highly prized in inland markets. In the early 17th century, a significant amount of the Ming's overseas silver flowed to Northeast China through the ginseng and sable fur trade. The Jurchen Aisin Gioro family, who had served as military commanders in the region for generations, accumulated considerable wealth from this trade.

The Ming dynasty fell to the peasant rebellion led by Li Zicheng (1606–1645), but it was the Aisin Gioro family who ultimately established a new dynasty on its ruins. Starting with Nurhaci (1559–1626) (fig. 101), the Aisin Gioro family used the wealth acquired from trade with the Ming to purchase firearms and hire skilled officers, quickly rising to prominence amid the tribal conflicts in the northeast. Centering on the Jurchens, Nurhaci gathered a mixed military and civilian force that included Jurchens, Mongols, Koreans, and Han Chinese, and founded the Eight Banners, a military and administrative organization that transcended tribal affiliations. During their campaigns, they formed close and stable marital and alliance relationships with the Mongols, establishing control over the steppes in North China. Most of the Qing emperors' consorts were Mongol noblewomen. In 1636, Nurhaci's eighth son, Huang Taiji (1592–1643), declared himself emperor in Shenyang, present-day Liaoning Province in Northeast China, naming the state the Great Qing, thus formally challenging the Ming dynasty. In 1644, amidst the chaos caused by Li Zicheng's rebellion, the Qing army entered the Central Plains through Shanhai Pass (the easternmost stronghold along the Ming Great Wall), overthrowing the Ming dynasty (fig. 102). The vast pastoral and agricultural regions were once again unified under a single dynasty with its capital in the Central Plains.

The pastoral and agricultural regions were complementary in terms of economic resources and political characteristics, but mishandling them could easily lead to ethnic oppression and regional conflicts. Learning from history, the Qing rulers designed a system that leveraged the traditional Chinese concept of unification. They integrated diverse traditions from the Northeast, Mongolia, Tibet, and Xinjiang into their cultural order, achieving long-term stable multi-ethnic governance. The Qing emperors adopted multiple identities—Emperor, Khan, Chakravartin, and the incarnation of Manjushri—based on the unique beliefs and customs of each ethnic group, thereby solidifying the legitimacy of their dynasty (fig. 103).

Fig. 103 *A Royal Banquet at Wanshuyuan* (detail)

Giuseppe Castiglione (1688–1766)
Ink and color on silk
Length 419.6 cm, height 221.2 cm (for full scroll)
The Palace Museum, Beijing

This painting depicts Emperor Qianlong hosting a banquet for Mongolian tribal leaders at the Wanshuyuan in the Chengde Mountain Resort (located in present-day Chengde, Hebei Province). It reflects the Qing dynasty's governance of frontier ethnic groups.

2. The Local Gentry

Zhu Yuanzhang, who came from a poor peasant background, took measures against powerful landlords and encouraged land-holding peasants to cultivate wastelands. With a simple egalitarian vision, he aimed to build a nation with a self-sufficient peasant economy as its foundation. During the Ming

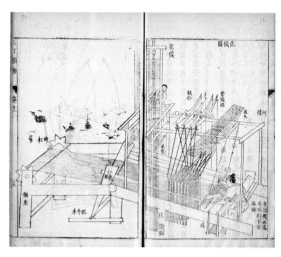

Fig. 104 Craftsmen weaving silk, as depicted in *The Exploitation of the Works of Nature (Tiangong Kaiwu)*, authored by Song Yingxing, a prominent scientist and encyclopedist of the Ming dynasty. The book documents various ancient Chinese technologies before the mid-Ming dynasty, including techniques for spinning, dyeing, and the cultivation of rice.

and Qing periods, the governments hoped that the populace would remain committed to their traditional occupations, such as land-holding peasants, craftsmen (fig. 104), and soldiers, passing these roles down through generations to maintain the stable operation of the state. However, this ideal picture was soon shattered by the shifting reality. The princes, high-ranking officials, and influential eunuchs seized large amounts of land. Especially notable were the gentry, who participated in the imperial examinations, held official titles, enjoyed tax exemptions, and had political privileges. They gained significant advantages in land acquisition and became crucial local elites in grassroots society. By the mid to late Ming dynasty, the burgeoning market economy also saw many prosperous merchants joining their ranks. The influence of local elites on local governments grew increasingly strong, and consulting with the gentry became a necessary procedure for local officials when making major decisions regarding local governance and reforms.

At the same time, clans and various civil organizations began to flourish. By leading these organizations, local elites controlled grassroots wealth, infrastructure, and public opinion. Among these, the most important were the clans, linked by blood ties. The local gentry usually served as the leaders within the clans, representing the clans externally to protect their interests and mediating internal conflicts among members. To sustain their operations, clans generally held communal property. Expenses for supporting clan members in taking the imperial examinations, assisting families in need, and building public infrastructure were all covered by communal funds. Families with a tradition of commerce would also use communal property as capital for business ventures. For example, the mining of copper in Yunnan and Guizhou provinces (inland provinces in southwestern China), the production of well salt in southern Sichuan Province, and the operation of coal mines around Beijing all relied on clans to pool substantial capital for large-scale operations. In this sense, clans can be seen as company organizations with Chinese characteristics.

Frequent commercial travel and increased social mobility during the Ming and Qing periods led to the formation of various mutual aid organizations. In the early Ming dynasty, it became common for officials from the same hometown to establish guild halls in the capital to provide food, lodging, and financial support for local candidates taking the imperial examinations (fig. 105). Merchants imitated this practice by setting up hometown guild halls in places where they resided, serving as venues for fellow townspeople to meet, discuss matters, and provide charitable services. As a result, guild halls were established across the country in major cities and commercial ports. When newcomers arrived in a place, they often first settled through their hometown guild halls, where they could establish social connections. Since merchants from the same place often engaged in the same trade in a particular area, many hometown guild halls also functioned

Fig. 105 The Shanxi-Shaanxi Guild Hall, built in Sheqi County, Henan Province by merchants from Shanxi and Shaanxi provinces during the Qing dynasty, served the local merchants from the same hometowns. It houses a shrine to the war god Guan Yu, revered for protecting merchants and travelers.

as trade guilds. Additionally, there were trade-specific guild halls for various industries, such as rice, medicine, and tea, which coordinated competition and protected the interests of the industry.

The Ming and Qing governments took a two-pronged approach to civil organizations: while they supported them as extensions of the government's social management functions, they also closely monitored them for any signs of developing into political factions. For instance, certain literary and poetry societies, initially formed by scholars for academic discourse and preparation for imperial examinations, faced suppression when they developed into political organizations and became entangled with political movements and court conflicts.

China's population surged from 60 million to 400 million during the Ming and Qing dynasties, yet the number of bureaucrats failed to keep pace. As the socio-economic landscape evolved, local affairs became more intricate and demanding. The tension between centralized small governments and the mounting public affairs found temporary relief through the intervention of the gentry.

By the middle to late Qing dynasty, spurred by urban prosperity, particularly the growth of trading ports in the late Qing period, many gentries migrated to urban areas, gradually diminishing their mass base in rural regions. The influx of machine-produced foreign goods in the late Qing era disrupted local agriculture and handicrafts, undermining the traditional economic footing of the gentry. Simultaneously, foreign influences and internal upheavals presented unprecedented challenges to the Qing government, exposing the inadequacies of the small government model bolstered by the gentry, which had prevailed throughout Ming and Qing China. The demise of imperial China and the advent of modern governance unfolded amidst the pressures of these monumental shifts.

Fig. 106 The archway cluster in Shexian, Anhui Province, showcases the glory of Huizhou merchant families.

Commerce and Urbanization

During the Ming and Qing periods, the population experienced significant growth. In the Yangtze River Delta, traditionally a major rice-producing region, there was a shift in land use towards more lucrative crops like mulberry and cotton for silk and fabric production, while grain cultivation moved to the middle and upper reaches of the Yangtze River. By the middle Ming dynasty, crops such as maize, sweet potatoes, and potatoes, introduced from the Americas and suitable for cultivation in mountainous terrain, enabled farmers to cultivate previously uncultivated areas. Products such as tea and timber from these mountainous regions found markets across the country. The opening of new lands and changes in production structures fostered the growth of commerce, which, in turn, brought about profound changes in Chinese society through the redistribution of resources and wealth.

1. Merchant Groups

The long-distance transportation of commodities required a significant investment of capital. For market-oriented products such as cotton cloth and tea, capital was needed not only during the transportation stage but also for raw material production and product manufacturing. Merchants must provide upfront capital, as producers would otherwise lack the funds and be reluctant to self-finance production without a confirmed purchase commitment. Blood ties and geographical connections became the primary channels through which merchants gathered capital and established credit.

During the Ming and Qing periods, numerous regional merchant groups based on clan and blood relations emerged, with the Shanxi merchants and the Huizhou (from present-day Huangshan and surrounding areas in the southern part of Anhui Province) merchants (fig. 106)

Fig. 107 Ancient Pingyao City in the central Shanxi Province, now the most intact ancient county city in China, was a gathering place for merchants and their exchange firms.

being the most well-known. These regions, characterized by mountainous terrain and limited arable land, were not suitable for efficient agriculture, prompting many residents to engage in commerce. They pooled capital through partnerships or by accepting entrusted funds, leveraging clan and local connections to invest in trade.

The government also relied on merchants for large-scale logistical operations. For instance, the Ming government gathered military provisions on the northern frontier with the financial assistance of the Shanxi and Huizhou merchants. In return, these merchants obtained the rights to transport and sell salt, traditionally a government monopoly, allowing them to amass substantial wealth. With robust capital backing, Shanxi and Huizhou merchants not only participated extensively in the long-distance trade of goods such as cotton cloth and tea, but also organized financial services like pawnshops and draft banks, thereby activating societal

wealth (fig. 107).

In traditional Chinese society, merchants were often relegated to a lower social status due to the perception that they did not directly contribute to wealth creation. However, during the Ming and Qing dynasties, the success of merchants began to challenge this belief. Shanxi merchants, for instance, preferred to send their most talented sons into business, as they found that managing a pawnshop could be more financially rewarding than pursuing a career in the civil service through passing the imperial examinations. Other options for career paths included seeking minor government positions or joining the military, with formal education being the least favored choice.

In contrast, Huizhou merchants advocated for a dual path of commerce and officialdom. They placed emphasis on providing their children with early education, with a contingency plan of

transitioning into business if they failed the imperial examinations. Alternatively, siblings might pursue different paths, with some entering politics and others engaging in business, supporting each other along the way. Recognizing that major trades such as salt were subject to government regulation, Huizhou merchants prioritized success in the imperial exams to enhance their relationships with the authorities. Qianlong (reigned 1736–1795), the sixth emperor of the Qing dynasty, undertook multiple tours to southern China, where Huizhou salt merchants spared no expense in lavishly welcoming the emperor to gain favor and advance their interests.

2. Refined Lifestyle

When Shanxi and Huizhou merchants first emerged, most of them were very thrifty. However, as wealth accumulated, their lifestyle tended towards extravagance. Initially, they constructed magnificent residences and gardens (fig. 108), flaunting luxurious clothing and cuisine. Eventually, they pursued a refined and elegant lifestyle, requiring not only financial resources but also cultural refinement.

Merchants spared no expense in acquiring and collecting ancient books, paintings, and antiques. They invited scholars to utilize their collections for academic research, thus

Fig. 108 The Slender West Lake Scenic Area in Yangzhou, Jiangsu Province. It was constructed by salt merchants from Huizhou during the Qing dynasty. The Five Pavilion Bridge on the right side was built to welcome Emperor Qianlong. Resembling a lotus flower, it is also known as the Lotus Bridge and is now a landmark of the Slender West Lake.

earning esteem and camaraderie among intellectuals. Among them, the salt merchants of Huizhou were particularly renowned. Many distinguished scholars in the periods of Emperor Qianlong and Emperor Jiaqing (reigned 1796–1820) were esteemed guests of these salt merchants. During the Qianlong era, when the government compiled the extensive series of books covering fields such as literature, history, and philosophy, known as the *Siku Quanshu* (*Complete Library of the Four Treasuries*), many rare books were acquired from the private collections of Huizhou salt merchants.

The Huizhou salt merchants residing around Yangzhou (in present-day eastern coastal province Jiangsu) also nurtured the tradition of supporting opera troupes. Given Emperor Qianlong's fondness for opera, they specifically selected Anhui opera troupes to perform in the capital. The performances of these troupes were highly esteemed by the nobility, gentry, and scholar-officials in Beijing. Incorporating various regional operatic styles, such as Kun opera from Kunshan in Jiangsu Province and Qinqiang opera from Shaanxi Province, the performers created a rich tapestry of influences. By the end of the Qing dynasty, these diverse influences coalesced into a distinctive

theatrical genre known as Peking Opera. Rapidly gaining popularity nationwide, it became China's most influential form of theater, earning the title of the country's "national opera" (fig. 109).

The economic growth also afforded people the chance to embrace a more refined lifestyle. In the late Ming period, there was a surge in tourism among both the literati and common folk. They embarked on journeys to admire picturesque landscapes with friends and acquaintances, often immortalizing these experiences through poetry and prose. One notable destination was Mount Huangshan, situated in the homeland of Huizhou merchants, which became a favored spot for tourists in the late Ming dynasty. This is related to the fact that Huizhou merchants invited many literati to visit the mountain and create poems.

To cater to travelers' needs, portable carrying cases and stoves were devised. The carrying case featured drawers and compartments for utensils and dishes, accommodating up to many people. The stove, equipped with charcoal and a copper pot, served for boiling water and heating

dishes en route. The carrying case and stove could be combined for convenience in transportation. Additionally, folding wooden tables were crafted, with larger ones for serving food and wine, and smaller ones for burning incense and arranging flowers. Coupled with flexible and cozy blankets, travelers could indulge in a meal while marveling at the scenery.

Zhang Wu Zhi (also known as *Treatise on Superfluous Things*), a classic work of aestheticism in daily life from the late Ming dynasty written by Wen Zhenheng (1585–1645), a Ming dynasty scholar, painter, landscape garden designer, showcases the refined lifestyles and aesthetic tastes of Chinese literati. It covers various aspects such as residential gardens, furniture arrangements (fig. 110), transportation, clothing and jewelry, as well as vegetables and fruits. Offering guidance on selecting daily utensils, curios to display in the study, creating both beautiful and practical clothing, choosing flowers for the garden, raising fish in ponds, and acquiring worthy varieties of incense and tea, the book serves as a guide for elegant living through its eloquent prose.

Fig. 109 These are thirteen well-known late Qing dynasty Peking Opera actors with costume and makeup. In the Peking Opera, the appearance of characters is designed according to their gender, personality, age, profession, and social status, resulting in distinct facial makeup for each role.

Fig. 110 Ming dynasty armchair with a circular backrest housed in Shanghai Museum.

3. Urban Prosperity

The expansion of the commodity economy during the Ming and Qing periods caused a significant portion of the rural population to transition towards commerce and handicrafts in urban areas, fueling a surge in urbanization. Following Zhu Di's relocation of the capital to Beijing in the early Ming dynasty, extensive construction projects were initiated to expand upon the Yuan dynasty's capital. Transformed, Beijing served as the imperial capital throughout the subsequent Qing dynasty as well.

The area within Beijing's Second Ring Road today roughly corresponds to the Beijing city of the Ming and Qing dynasties. Divided by Qianmen Avenue, present-day Beijing was split into two parts during those periods. The northern part, known as the "inner city," was centered around the Forbidden City where the emperor resided, surrounded by government offices, royal residences, and imperial gardens. The southern part, the "outer city," was where commoners lived. It was a bustling commercial area, where various regional guild halls were clustered. In addition to domestic

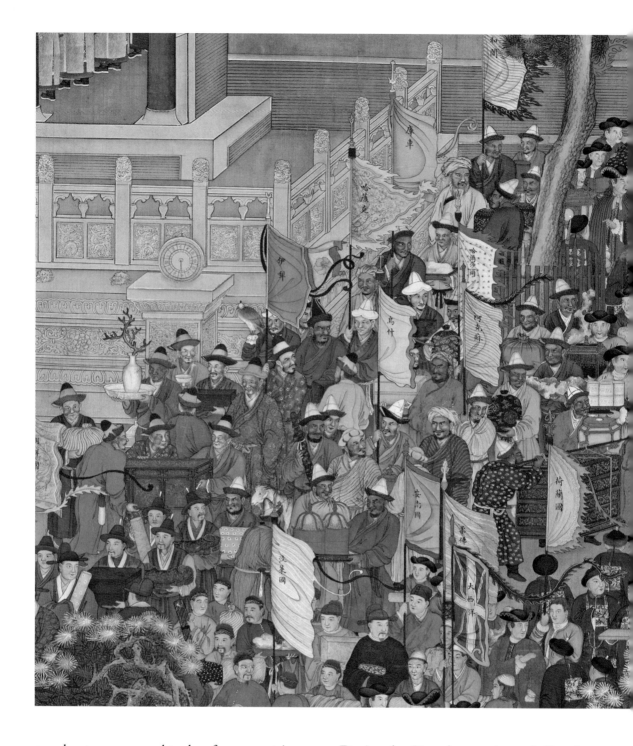

merchants, envoys and traders from countries such as Korea, Russia, Vietnam, and Ryukyu (modern-day Okinawa) gathered in Beijing (fig. 111). The Ming and Qing governments allowed foreign diplomatic missions to engage in trade with Chinese merchants after completing their tribute missions, and as a result, goods with exotic flavors were highly sought after by Chinese merchants.

During the Qing dynasty, it was believed that there were four most commercialized cities in the country: Beijing in the north, Foshan in Guangdong in the south, Suzhou in Jiangsu in the east, and Hankou in Hubei in the west. Among these cities, Suzhou was considered the most prosperous. Known as Gusu in ancient times, Suzhou was renowned for its developed handicraft industry in the

eastern half of the city, while the western half, adjacent to the Grand Canal, was renowned for its thriving commerce. In the 24th year of the Qianlong reign (1759), a palace artist painted a long scroll entitled *Prosperous Suzhou*, which was over 10 meters long and meticulously depicted the bustling scenes of Suzhou. Roughly counted, there were over 12,000 figures of various characters in the

Fig. 111 *Tribute of the Myriad Nations* (detail)

Anonymous (Qing dynasty)
Ink and color on silk
Length 207 cm, height 299 cm
The Palace Museum, Beijing

This is painted during the Qianlong era of the Qing dynasty, where envoys with different appearance and temperament from various countries and nationalities are dressed in colorful attires. The complete scroll is on page 6.

▲ **Fig. 112** *Prosperous Suzhou* (detail)
Xu Yang (Qing dynasty)
Ink and color on paper
Length 1,225 cm, height 35.8 cm
Liaoning Provincial Museum

The painting depicts the bustling Shantang Street,
Suzhou, one of the commercial centers in China in
the Qing dynasty. A detail is enlarged in the lower
right corner on the facing page.

▶ **Fig. 113** The present night view of Shantang
Street in Suzhou, Jiangsu Province.

painting, and nearly 400 boats, including
official, cargo, and passenger vessels. The
most striking feature of the painting was the
rows of shops along the streets, with signs
hanging high above the doors. Over 260
identifiable signs of various kinds of shops
were depicted, including those selling silk,
cotton fabric, mats, clothing, and jewelry
(fig. 112). The street scenes from Xumen to
Shantang Street depicted in *Prosperous Suzhou*
have been preserved to this day and have
become a popular tourist destination in the
old city of Suzhou (fig. 113).

During the urbanization wave of the
Ming and Qing periods, the most distinctive

development was the rise of small towns centered around commerce. These towns originated from ancient rural markets subordinate to counties. When these rural markets, which initially operated on fixed dates, began to open daily to meet market demand, they evolved into small towns. Small towns typically served the surrounding countryside, acting as distribution points for external goods to rural areas and gathering rural products for distribution to nearby regions. Some of these towns specialized in certain goods for the market, such as towns in southern China that focused on cotton and silk industries. Their trade networks extended beyond their immediate vicinity to other provinces.

Some of these towns grew into national economic centers. Among the four most prosperous cities in the eyes of the Qing people, Foshan and Hankou were not the original administrative centers of the region. Along with Jingdezhen in Jiangxi Province in southeastern China, known for its porcelain production even today, and Zhuxian Town in Henan Province, these towns were renowned for their thriving commerce and were collectively referred to as the "four great towns" during the Ming and Qing periods.

Challenges from a New World

After replacing the Yuan dynasty, the Ming dynasty had ambitions and actions to occupy the northern steppes. However, it had to contend with the nomadic powers along the Great Wall, where conflict and exchange coexisted. The Qing dynasty, through alliances and intermarriage between the Manchu and Mongol peoples, controlled present-day Mongolia but still faced challenges from nomadic powers in the Eurasian interior. Meanwhile, in the southeastern maritime direction, both the Ming and Qing dynasties encountered challenges from Japan and Europe. Conflict, though violent, can be seen as an alternative expression of the desire for exchange. Through conflicts and exchanges with other powers, China came to better understand the world and itself.

1. Beyond the Great Wall

The political landscape in the steppes of North China changed significantly after the Yuan dynasty retreated there. While the Ming dynasty maintained a long-standing standoff with northern nomadic forces along the Great Wall, the Oirat tribe emerged as the dominant power amidst the infighting among the Mongol tribes. As the core of the tribal alliance, the Oirats leveraged trade with the Ming dynasty to obtain resources, significantly boosting their power in the steppe conflicts. They once unified the Mongol tribes and demanded the Yuan dynasty's imperial regalia from the Ming, signaling their intent to restore the Yuan dynasty. This action led the Ming to halt trade between the two sides. Deprived of Ming resources, the Oirat tribe lost the economic foundation to sustain a vast nomadic khanate, leading to its rapid disintegration amid the collapse of the tribal alliance.

However, the economies of the nomadic and agrarian regions had become so interdependent that trade between them could no longer be halted. During the reign of the Jiajing Emperor (1522–1566), the Ming court once again accepted tribute from the nomadic tribes and reopened border trade. This measure catered to the demand for exchange between the two regions, resulting in long-lasting peace along the Great Wall.

During the Qing dynasty, the Mongols and Manchus maintained a long-standing alliance through intermarriage, transforming the Great Wall into a mere ecological boundary rather than a political divide. However, a branch of the Mongols, the Zunghar tribe, migrated west and established the powerful Zunghar Khanate in the vast lands between Lake Balkhash and the Selenga River. The nomadic Zunghars expanded their territory by attacking, instigating, and persuading various Mongol tribes under Qing control, eventually advancing into present-day Qinghai in northwestern China and Xizang in southwestern China. Through prolonged warfare during the reigns of Kangxi (reigned 1662–1722), Yongzheng (reigned 1723–1735), and Qianlong (reigned 1736–1795), the Qing dynasty capitalized on internal strife during a succession crisis within the Zunghar Khanate, ultimately defeating them. This victory allowed the Qing to gain complete control over the regions north and south of the Tianshan Mountains, stabilizing China's western frontier. The Qing Empire's powerful and stable logistical support from the agrarian regions enabled its victory over the Zunghar Khanate, the last nomadic khanate in the world (fig. 114).

2. Beyond the Coastline

The highly developed maritime trade of the Yuan dynasty was discontinued during the early Ming period under Zhu Yuanzhang's rule to prevent anti-government forces in exile from returning. The Yongle Emperor,

Fig. 114 A battle field where a Zunghar army was defeated by a Qing army.

Zhu Di, dispatched admiral Zheng He on seven voyages to distant lands, reaching as far as the East African coast (fig. 115). While these voyages were a remarkable achievement in the history of ancient Chinese navigation, they were primarily focused on extending the Ming tribute system rather than promoting overseas trade.

Against the backdrop of maritime prohibition, the Ming dynasty shifted from the Yuan dynasty's hostile relationship with Japan to establishing diplomatic ties. The government allowed the Japanese Ashikaga shogunate to send tribute missions to China, but only with certificates issued by the Ming court and limited to one mission every ten years. This restriction fell far short of meeting market demand. Consequently, the Ming dynasty's demand for maritime trade was bound to show up in another form, that is, various goods were smuggled from Japan, leading to rampant piracy. The Ming court later realized that the demand for maritime trade among the people should only be

Fig. 115 A model of a junk in Zheng He's fleet.

channeled, not blocked. Eventually, in 1567, the Ming government lifted the maritime prohibition, allowing registered merchants to engage in overseas trade with proper certification.

With the lifting of the maritime prohibition, the Ming dynasty soon encountered surprise visitors from beyond the East Asian tributary system. As Europe entered the Age of Exploration, Portuguese and Spanish galleons arrived at the southern and southeastern coasts of China seeking trade opportunities. Jesuit missionaries like Matteo Ricci (1552–1610), Lazzaro Cattaneo (1560–1640), and Nicolas Trigault (1577–1628) traveled on merchant ships, landing in places like Macau and eventually reaching inland China. Initially, the Jesuits faced repeated setbacks in their missionary efforts. However, they later attempted to accommodate Chinese customs and traditional ethics, studying Confucian classics and wearing scholar-official attire. This approach enabled them to integrate into the social circles of the scholar-officials.

Matteo Ricci presented religious icons and other gifts to the Wanli Emperor (reigned 1573–1620), but the emperor showed no interest in the religious items, only considering a self-striking clock he received as an amusing toy. Nevertheless, the books Ricci brought about astronomy, geography, and mathematics deeply fascinated many scholar-officials. Captivated by the scientific knowledge demonstrated by Lazzaro Cattaneo and Matteo Ricci, Xu Guangqi (1562–1633), a native of Shanghai, converted to Christianity and, with the help of Ricci and other missionaries, translated several books on geometry and astronomy (fig. 116). Meanwhile, the Jesuits translated and introduced Confucian classics to Europe.

Portuguese, Spanish, and Dutch traders who arrived in China in the early 17th century had extensive interactions with various powers in China and East Asia. As

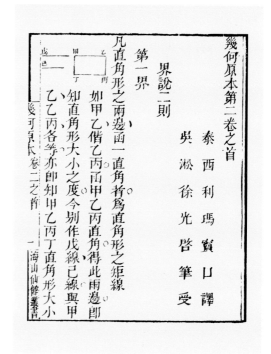

Fig. 116 A page of the Chinese edition of *Euclid's Elements*, translated by Xu Guangqi with the help of Matteo Ricci.

a result, the maritime trade relations during the late Ming and early Qing periods became intricate and complex. The Hongyipao (red barbarian cannons) introduced by European traders were highly sought after by all parties involved and played a crucial role in the conflicts during the transition from the Ming to Qing dynasties.

The rise of the Qing dynasty benefited from this trade; Emperor Kangxi lifted the maritime prohibition during his reign. Traders from Japan, Korea, Southeast Asia, India, and Europe maintained enduring commercial relations with China, forming a triangular trade route with intermediaries like India and Southeast Asia. China exported silk, tea, and porcelain, while receiving substantial amounts of silver from the Americas and Japan. Coastal provinces like Fujian and Guangzhou responded to both domestic and international demands by cultivating economic crops such as tea (fig. 117) and sugarcane. They supplemented these with rice imports from Southeast Asia to meet local needs. Initially, European merchant ships were permitted to

Fig. 117 A boat is loaded with packages of tea in Guangzhou in 1852.

trade in cities like Guangzhou and Ningbo. However, in the mid-18th century, British East India Company merchant James Flint engaged in unauthorized trade with Huizhou merchants in Ningbo. Consequently, the Qing court restricted European ships to trade solely in Guangzhou and limited transactions to designated agents appointed by the government.

At that time, the Qing government had yet to realize that these European merchants, arriving by sea with strong trade ambitions, would bring about changes to China unseen in nearly 3,000 years. Between 1792 and 1793, the British East India Company sponsored the Macartney Mission to China, aiming to expand trade. However, Emperor Qianlong, content with the self-sufficiency of the tributary trade system, showed no interest in connecting these circles to form a global trade network. In the mid-19th century, driven by capital, European nations used opium and gunboats to force open China's doors. This led to war reparations, trade deficits, and silver outflows that destroyed China's monetary system. The ensuing economic

crisis sparked political unrest, culminating in the Taiping Rebellion, a peasant war that broke out in southern China and spread across half the country. In response, the Qing government encouraged the adoption of advanced technology from abroad, initiating state-led early industrialization efforts and making substantial investments in advanced gunboats to establish a modern navy. However, repeated failures in diplomacy and domestic policies highlighted the Qing dynasty's inadequate capacity and efficiency as a nation.

Winning over agrarian states and nomadic confederations, the Qing dynasty forged a unified multi-ethnic nation, blending diverse ecological regions. Nevertheless, its political and economic systems and governing abilities proved lacking compared to contemporary state models. Faced with internal and external pressures, deep-seated social forces, including clans, merchant guilds, enterprises and other traditional or modern forms mobilized to address national shortcomings, paving the way for a revival of China's state structure in the 20th century.

門閶

Coda

The formation of China, a country with a long history and an early-maturing civilization, benefits from the fertile lands of East Asia, which were suitable for early human life, as well as from the adaptability of its people to diverse geographical environments and surrounding worlds. From the very beginning, China's history has been a series of dramas about how people from different geographical regions interact, coexist, communicate, and integrate. Even today, how to handle interpersonal relationships remains a central theme in the daily lives of Chinese people. This is also why we often regard China as a relation-based society.

Just like other regions of the world, China went through an era dominated by theocracy. However, even before the imperial era, the light of humanistic rationality had already begun to permeate Chinese thought and culture. As a result, Chinese

On pages 162–165

Figs. 118–119 Details of *Prosperous Suzhou*. Refer to fig. 112 on pages 156–157 for more information of the painting.

people place greater importance on earthly life and the recording of history, as they consider it the most valuable guide for living better in the present.

Equally valued by the Chinese are the concepts of nation and family. China as a nation, and Chinese identity, were formed over such a long historical period that the collective memory is deeply ingrained. This enduring historical consciousness evokes a profound sense of patriotism and familial loyalty among the Chinese people.

Lastly, let us express our gratitude to the ancient Chinese historian officials who, born in such rich historical and cultural soil, have preserved for us the world's oldest and most continuous historical records. Through their efforts, we understand what China is and what it means to be Chinese—a people with a unique perception of and feelings about history.

APPENDICES

DATES OF THE CHINESE DYNASTIES

Xia Dynasty（夏）..2070–1600 BC

Shang Dynasty（商）..1600–1046 BC

Zhou Dynasty（周）..1046–256 BC

    Western Zhou Dynasty（西周）................................1046–771 BC

    Eastern Zhou Dynasty（东周）................................770–256 BC

        The Spring and Autumn Period（春秋）...........770–476 BC

        The Warring States Period（战国）.................475–221 BC

Qin Dynasty（秦）...221–206 BC

Han Dynasty（汉）...202 BC–AD 220

    Western Han Dynasty（西汉）.................................202 BC–AD 8

    Xin Dynasty（新朝）..8–23

    Eastern Han Dynasty（东汉）.................................25–220

Three Kingdoms（三国）...220–280

    Wei（魏）...220–265

    Shu Han（蜀）..221–263

    Wu（吴）..221–280

Jin Dynasty（晋）..265–420

    Western Jin Dynasty（西晋）..................................265–316

    Eastern Jin Dynasty（东晋）..................................317–420

    Sixteen Kingdoms（十六国）...................................304–439

Northern and Southern Dynasties（南北朝）.................420–589

    Southern Dynasties（南朝）....................................420–589

    Northern Dynasties（北朝）....................................439–581

Sui Dynasty（隋）..581–618

Tang Dynasty（唐）..618–907

Five Dynasties and Ten Kingdoms（五代十国）...............907–979

    Five Dynasties（五代）..907–960

    Ten Kingdoms（十国）..902–979

Song Dynasty（宋）..960–1279

    Northern Song Dynasty（北宋）...............................960–1126

    Southern Song Dynasty（南宋）..............................1127–1276

Liao Dynasty（辽）..916–1125

Western Xia Dynasty (Tangut)（西夏）..........................1038–1227

Jin Dynasty（金）..1115–1234

Yuan Dynasty（元）..1271–1368

Ming Dynasty（明）..1368–1644

Qing Dynasty（清）..1644–1911

INDEX